Meditation, Transformation, and Dream Yoga

by Ven. Gyatrul Rinpoche

Translations by
Sangye Khandro
and B. Alan Wallace

Snow Lion Publications
Ithaca, New York
Boulder, Colorado

Snow Lion Publications
P.O. Box 6483
Ithaca, New York 14851 USA
(607) 273-8519
www.snowlionpub.com

Second Edition USA 2002

Printed in USA on acid-free, recycled paper.

This edition ISBN 1-55939-183-9

The Library of Congress catalogued the previous edition of this
book as follows:

Gyatrul, Rinpoche, 1924-
     Ancient wisdom: Nyingma teachings on dream yoga, meditation
and transformation / Gyatrul Rinpoche. – 1st ed.
          p. cm.
     "Root text translations by B. Alan Wallace. "
     "Commentary translations by Sangye Khandro."
     Contents: Transforming felicity and adversity into the spiritual
path / by Jigme Tenpe Nyima – Releasing oneself from essential
delusion / by Lochen Dharma Shri – The illumination of primordial
wisdom / by His Holiness Dudjom Rinpoche.
     ISBN 1-55939-018-2
     1. Spiritual life Rñiṅ-ma-pa (Sect) 2. Rñiṅ-ma-pa (Sect) –
Doctrines. I. Jigme Tenpe Nyima. Skyid sdug lam 'khyer bshugs so.
English. 1993. II. Lochen Dharma Shri. Rdor sems thugs kyi sgrub
pa'i rmi lam gyi khrid yig zin bris su spel ba nying 'khrul ran grol.
English. 1993 III. Dudjom, Rinpoche. Bdud 'dul dbang drag rdo rje
gro lod kyi rdzogs rim ka dag gi khrid yig ye shes snang ba.
English. 1993. IV. Wallace, B. Alan. V. Khandro, Sangye. VI. Title.
BQ7662.6.G93   1993
234.3'444—dc20   93-13992
                                                              CIP

Contents

Introduction

If we were to consider condensing all Dharma practices and required daily commitments into the most essential practices necessary to accomplish realization in this immediate lifetime, we must then consider our own time and how it is spent. A slot of time is usually dedicated to a daily practice or routine of formal practice. Most of the daytime is spent involved in various activities with family, friends and in the job place. Finally there is the time that we spend sleeping and dreaming during the night. It is with these three time periods in mind that the three texts were chosen for this book. Each of these three texts and their commentaries give the methods and practical instructions that are applicable to these times so that our goal of liberation in this very life can be achieved.

First, *Transforming Felicity and Adversity into the Spiritual Path* by Jigme Tenpe Nyima was selected as the contemporary classic for improving the quality of daily life experiences and teaching the precise methods through which extremes can be brought to the path. This new English translation by B. Alan Wallace is illuminating and superb.

The second selection, *Releasing Oneself from Essential Delusion* by Lochen Dharma Shri, is one of the most direct and useful dream yoga accomplishment manuals available. Translated from the original Tibetan by B. Alan Wallace, it is as clear as it is precise. The commentary to it presented here was taught by Gyatrul Rinpoche during the summer of 1990 in Ashland, Oregon.

The third selection, *The Illumination of Primordial Wisdom* by H.H. Dudjom Rinpoche, again is one of the most simple, direct and useful manuals on ascertaining the view, meditation and conduct through the Great Perfection practices of quiescence and insight (*śamatha* and *vipassana*). This teaching is meant to be accomplished in formal sitting sessions and carried into daily life experience.

Even if we are successful in our formal practice and lucid dream awareness, if our daily life experiences are still the cause of hope and fear – thus increasing our excitement and disappointment – then the goal of liberation in this life is impaired. This little key to the transformation of all highs and lows into true spiritual awareness is truly indispensable.

The commentary to this text was given by Gyatrul Rinpoche to the Vajradhatu community at Boulder, Colorado in the fall of 1991. Hours before the teaching was scheduled to begin, we received the sad news of the parinirvana of H.H. Dilgo Khyentse Rinpoche in Thimphu, Bhutan. The impact of this news, combined with the subject material, was yet another miraculous display of the guru's kindness.

I would like to thank B. Alan Wallace for the excellent translation he has made of the three root texts. In the twenty years that we have known one another as dharma friends, Alan has always been a source of knowledge and an inspiration, as well as a good friend.

I would also like to thank Kay Henry for all the effort she has put into the preparation of this manuscript. Her enthusiasm to work hard for the Dharma is a source of joy.

— *Sangye Khandro*
Tashi Chöling
August, 1992

PART I
TRANSFORMATION

Transforming Felicity and Adversity into the Spiritual Path
by
**Jigme Tenpe Nyima,
The Third Dodrupchen Rinpoche**

Translated by
B. Alan Wallace

**Commentary by
Venerable Gyatrul Rinpoche**

Translated by
Sangye Khandro

*Part 1   The Root Text
by Jigme Tenpe Nyima,
The Third Dodrupchen Rinpoche*

Transforming Felicity and Adversity into the Spiritual Path

Homage:

Oh, Noble Avalokiteshvara,
Who always rejoices at the happiness of others,
Who is deeply saddened by others' suffering,
Who has perfectly realized the qualities of great
    compassion,
And who has released his own joy and sorrow...

I bow to you recalling your virtues; and I shall explain in part the quintessential teaching on transforming felicity and adversity into the spiritual path, this being an indispensable tool of spiritually realized beings, which is invaluable in the world.

HOW TO TRANSFORM ADVERSITY INTO THE SPIRITUAL PATH BY MEANS OF RELATIVE TRUTH

Whenever you are afflicted by sentient beings or anything else, if you habituate your mind to dwelling on suffering only, even the most insignificant circumstance will bring forth great distress. This is because whatever attitude you cultivate towards felicity and adversity will, by nature, grow stronger. Thus, as the power of gradual habituation increases, eventually virtually everything that appears will lead to misery, and there will be no possibility of happiness.

By not recognizing that this is due to your own mental habits, you blame this on external circumstances, and eventually the flames of hatred, evil actions, suffering and so on spread endlessly. Thus, appearances arise as enemies. The reason why sentient beings of this corrupt era are afflicted by suffering stems from our interior powers of discrimination; so this calls for precise understanding.

Therefore, the meaning of not being afflicted by the hindrances of enemies, sickness, malevolent spirits, and so on is not that one averts the arising of illness, etc. or prevents their occurrence in the future. Rather, it means that these things are not able to arise as obstacles to following the spiritual path.

In order for this to happen, you must (1) dispense with the attitude of utter aversion to adversity and (2) develop the attitude of good cheer in the face of adversity.

*Dispensing with the Attitude of Utter Aversion
to Adversity*

Recognize again and again the pointlessness and great detriment of all the miserable anxiety you experience through regarding adversity as being purely unfavorable. And thoroughly accustom yourself to the powerful anticipation, "From now on, whatever kind of adversity arises, I shall not quail." In this way practice cultivating great courage.

The pointlessness of aversion to adversity. If adversity can be corrected, there is no need to be despondent; and, if it cannot be remedied, there is no benefit even if one becomes unhappy.

The great detriment of such aversion. If you do not react with anxiety, due to the strength of your mind, it will be easy to experience and handle even great adversity as if it were as light and flimsy as cotton wool. On the other hand, if you react with anxiety, you will become unbearably oppressed with overwhelming misery in the face of even minor adversity.

For example, while thinking about a gorgeous woman (or man), even if you try to stop desire, you just wear yourself out. Likewise, by engrossing yourself in the miserable aspects of some adverse situation, you will be unable to develop any sense of fortitude. Thus, as in the instructions on guarding the doors of the senses, in the event of adversity you should not become engrossed in its characteristics; rather, get used to placing your mind in its natural state and let it apprehend its own nature.

Developing a Sense of Good Cheer in the Face of Adversity

Cultivate a sense of good cheer by regarding adversity as an aid on the spiritual path. Moreover, for whatever kind of adversity arises, if you do not have individual practices to apply to each one in accordance with your own mental abilities, by merely having a theoretical understanding, you may simply think many times, "In general, if one is skillful, it's possible to attain such and such benefits as a result of adversity." But this will be like the saying, "Great is the distance between the sky and the earth." And it will be difficult for you to succeed. The goal is farther than the sky is from the earth.

Adversity as the support for training in the mind of emergence (renunciation) from samsara. Recognize that as long as you wander without self-control in the cycle of existence, the occurrence of such adversity is not an injustice or something unfair; rather, that is the very nature of the cycle of existence. Further, if it is difficult to bear even such minor adversity as this that is encountered occasionally in this fortunate realm of existence, there is no point in mentioning the adversities of the unfortunate realms. Develop a sense of disillusionment, thinking, "Alas! The cycle of existence is a bottomless and endless ocean of adversity!" and direct your attention towards liberation.

Adversity as the support for training in going for refuge. Practice going for refuge by contemplating with conviction, "For the repeated affliction of such fear as this throughout all my lives, the sole, unfailing refuge is the Three Jewels. So, whatever happens, I shall entrust myself to them alone and never abandon them under any circumstances."

Adversity as the support for dispelling arrogance. Bearing in mind the way in which you lack self-control, as explained previously, and the way in which you continuously fail to escape being controlled by adversity, snuff out the enemy of pride, which destroys prosperity, and the unwholesome attitude of holding others in contempt.

Adversity as the support for purifying unwholesome actions. Consider, "Such adversity as this, as well as immeasurably greater adversities, arise only as a result of unwholesome actions," and carefully ponder the four points that (1) actions invariably give rise to corresponding effects, (2) the effects of actions increase, (3) one never experiences the effects of actions that were not committed, and (4) deeds committed never fail to produce results. Thus, bear in mind, "If I don't want adversity, I must avoid its cause, which is non-virtue," and by means of the four powers disclose such actions that you have already amassed, and strive to restrain yourself in the future.

Adversity as the support for attraction to virtue. Ponder at length, "If I take delight in felicity, which is the opposite of adversity, I must strive for its cause, which is virtue," and in various ways do whatever you can to progress in the direction of virtue.

Adversity as the support for training in compassion. Reflect on the ways in which other sentient beings, like you, are afflicted with adversity like your own or even far greater, and train yourself in thinking, "May they, too, be free of all adversity!" This will also bring an understanding of how to cultivate loving-kindness for those who are bereft of happiness.

Adversity as the support for cultivating the attitude of cherishing others more than oneself. Cultivate the attitude, "The reason that I am not free of such adversity is that I have always been self-centered, so now I shall devote myself solely to the attitude of cherishing others, which is the source of happiness and prosperity."

When misfortune stares you in the face, it is very difficult, so it is crucial to become familiar with these practices beforehand, and to emphasize those in which you have the most vivid experience.

It is not enough for adversity to become an aid to your spiritual practice. Rather, it is vital that you cultivate a strong and continuous sense of gladness as a result of clearly recognizing that this is happening. So, whenever you apply what has been explained here, think such thoughts as this: "Such adversity is a great help to me in experiencing the many, wonderful joys of the higher realms that lead to liberation, which are extremely difficult to reach. By continuing in this way, even if my suffering is severe, it is extremely agreeable, like *ladu*, a sweetmeat the taste of which is both sweet and hot." Consider this point repeatedly and with care, and accustom yourself to a sense of good cheer.

By doing this, your abundant, or predominant, sense of mental well-being will make physical pain seem imperceptible. The inability of physical pain to afflict the mind is the criterion of being able to overcome illness by means of inner strength, and this suggests that this is also the criterion for overcoming enemies, malevolent spirits, and so on.

As explained above, reversing the attitude of antipathy towards adversity is the basis for causing adversity to arise as the spiritual path. For as long as your mind is troubled with anxiety and despair, it is impossible for adversity to be brought onto the path.

Moreover, by training in actually bringing adversity onto the path, you will encounter unprecedented benefits, for you will see for yourself how adversity can enhance your spiritual practice, and your sense of well-being will continue to increase.

It is said, "If you practice at first with minor adversity, it will gradually become easy; and, in this way, you will finally be able to practice even in the face of great adversity." This is what is needed, for it is difficult to reach an experience that is beyond the capacity of your own mind.

In between meditation sessions, pray to your spiritual mentor and the Three Jewels that adversity will arise as the spiritual path. When the power of your mind has increased somewhat, make offerings to the Three Jewels and other beings, with the supplication, "For the sake of empowering my spiritual practice, let there be unfavorable circumstances!" And at all times sustain a deep sense of good cheer.

When you first begin to practice, it is helpful to meditate far removed from distractions. For in the midst of distractions (1) you are liable to be diverted by many unwholesome companions who will ask you, "How can you put up with such adversity, contempt, and abuse?"; (2) worrying about enemies, relatives, and possessions will cloud and uncontrollably disturb your awareness, and you will slip into bad habits; and (3) furthermore, you will be carried away by all kinds of distracting situations.

In solitude your awareness will be very clear due to the absence of those things, so it is easy to set your mind to the task at hand. It is said that this is the very reason that, when those who engage in "cutting through" (*chöd*) train in the attitude of suppressing adversity, at first they put off applying the training, in the midst of distractions, to harm caused by humans. Instead, they emphasize applying this training to illusory manifestations of gods and demons in solitary cemeteries and wild habitats.

To sum up: In order not only to prevent all unfavorable circumstances and adversity from afflicting your mind, but to cause them to elicit a sense of good cheer, you should put a stop to experiences of aversion toward both inner and outer obstacles – illness as well as enemies, spirits, vicious gossip, etc. Practice seeing everything solely in an agreeable way. For that to happen, you should stop seeing those harmful situations as something wrong, but give all your effort to seeing them as valuable. For it is the way our minds apprehend situations that makes them agreeable or disagreeable. For example, those who reflect at length on the faults of worldly amusements become increasingly perturbed the more they are surrounded by admiring people and enjoyments; whereas those who regard worldly amusements as beneficial aspire to increase them.

By training in this way, you will become gentle-minded, easy-going, and courageous; there will be no obstacles to your spiritual practice; all unfavorable circumstances will arise as splendid and auspicious; and your mind will continually be content with the joy of serenity. To follow a spiritual path in a degenerate era, such armor as this is indispensable.

Then, since you are free of the suffering of anxiety, other types of misery also vanish, like weapons falling from the hands of soldiers; and even illnesses, etc. tend to disappear of their own accord. We can learn from the saints of the past who say, "By not becoming distressed at anything and not succumbing to unhappiness, your mind will not become troubled; since it is undisturbed, your nervous system will not become disturbed; due to that, the other elements of your body will not come into disequilibrium; as a result, your mind will not become troubled, etc., and the wheel of well-being spins on."

They also say, "Just as birds find horses and donkeys with sores on their backs easy prey, so do malevolent spirits find an easy target in people with fearful dispositions, but it is hard for them to overcome people of steady character."

Therefore, the wise see that all adversity and felicity depends on the mind, and they seek happiness within the mind. Since they have the complete causes of happiness within them, they do not rely on externals. They are not afflicted by the harms of sentient beings or anything else, and this remains true even at the time of death. They are always free.

In this way the bodhisattvas attain the "samadhi that suffuses all phenomena with well-being."

However, the foolish run after external objects in the hope of finding happiness, but whatever happiness they achieve, great or small, turns out like the saying, "It's not you who is in charge; your hair is caught up in a tree!" There is just one failure after another, due to things not working out, not coming together, occurring in disproportionate ways, etc. Enemies, thieves, and so on have ample opportunities to harm them, and even the slightest criticism separates them from their happiness. However much a crow looks after a baby cuckoo, the cuckoo can't become its own offspring. Just so, since their minds can never become steady, there is nothing but fatigue for the gods, affliction for the spirits, and misery for themselves. This is quintessential advice that comprises a hundred crucial points in one.

There are many other types of austerities for following the spiritual path by willingly accepting adversity, and other types of instructions, such as those in the *Zhijé* teachings, for bringing illness and harmful influences onto the path. But here I have offered an easily understandable, general discussion of accepting adversity, based on the treatises by the noble Shantideva and his wise followers.

HOW TO TRANSFORM ADVERSITY INTO THE SPIRITUAL PATH BY MEANS OF ULTIMATE TRUTH

With the instrument of such reasoning as the refutation of the "four extreme views concerning production," the mind is brought to the supreme peace of emptiness and abides there, in the nature of reality in which unfavorable circumstances and adversity, or even their names, are not to be found. Even when one rises from that state, adversity does not appear to the mind as it did earlier, when it would be experienced with fear, despair, and so on. Rather, adversity is overcome by regarding it as an assemblage of mere words. I shall not elaborate.

HOW TO TRANSFORM FELICITY INTO THE SPIRITUAL PATH BY MEANS OF RELATIVE TRUTH

When happiness and the objective conditions for happiness occur, if you fall under their control, arrogance, conceit, complacency, etc. will grow and obstruct your spiritual path. It is difficult not to succumb to their influence, for as Padampa Sangye said, "People can handle only a little felicity, but they can handle a lot of adversity."

Therefore, from various perspectives regard those things as impermanent and unsatisfactory, and cultivate a strong sense of disillusionment. Try to direct your mind away from carelessness and think, "Thus, all the pleasures of the world are trifling and are bound up with many problems. Nevertheless, some of them have good qualities. The Buddha said that, for a person whose freedom is impaired by suffering, it is very difficult to attain enlightenment; but one who abides in happiness attains enlightenment with great ease. The fact that I have the opportunity to practice dharma in such a state of happiness is great fortune. So, at this time I shall by all means convert my happiness into dharma; and since dharma also gradually gives rise to happiness, I shall practice making dharma and happiness complement each other. Otherwise, like boiling a drink in a wooden vessel, I will end up just where I started." You should grasp the essence by earnestly integrating whatever happiness you experience with dharma. This is the message of (Nagarjuna's) *Jewel Garland*.

Even when you are happy, by failing to recognize it you will not be able to use it for your dharma practice. So, as a remedy against devoting your whole life to a myriad of concerns and activities in the pursuit of just a bit more pleasure, recognize the agreeable as being agreeable, and devote yourself to the nectar of contentment.

There are other practices of bringing felicity onto the spiritual path, etc., based on contemplation of the kindness of the Three Jewels and on the instructions for cultivating a spirit of awakening, but this will do for now.

Resorting to solitude, you should alternately train in practices of accumulating (wisdom and merit) and of purification. The same is true of bringing adversity onto the path.

HOW TO TRANSFORM FELICITY INTO THE SPIRITUAL PATH BY MEANS OF ULTIMATE TRUTH

The practice by means of ultimate truth is to be understood from the previous explanation.

If you cannot practice dharma when you are sad, due to what this does to your mind, and you cannot practice dharma when you are happy, because you become attached to that, then there will be no time at all when you can practice dharma. So, if you are to practice dharma, there is nothing more useful than this. If you do have this practice, wherever you dwell, in solitude or in a city, whether you accompany good or bad companions, whether you are rich or poor, happy or sad, whether you hear praise or blame, or pleasant or unpleasant speech, since you are free from fear that any of this can bring you down, you respond in the manner of a lion-like yogi. Whatever you do, your mind will be cheerful and spacious, and your character will be pure and benevolent. Even if your body dwells in an impure land, your mind will frolic in the splendor of unimaginable joy, like a bodhisattva of a pure realm. This corresponds to the saying of the precious Kadampas:

> With happiness brought under control
> And sadness brought to an end,
> When you are lonely, this will be your
>   companion;
> When you are ill, this will be your nurse.

For example, a goldsmith purifies gold by melting it in fire and makes it malleable by rinsing it again and again in water. Likewise, by bringing felicity onto the path your mind will be subdued, and by bringing adversity onto the path, it will become pristine. When this happens, you will easily achieve extraordinary states of samadhi in which your body and mind will be perfectly fit for the tasks you set them. I feel that this is the most profound of instructions for perfecting moral discipline, which is the root of all that is good. By not being attached to felicity, you establish the basis for the special moral discipline of a renunciant;

and, by not being afraid of adversity, you fully purify that moral discipline. This is implied by the saying that generosity is the basis of moral discipline, and forbearance is the purifier of moral discipline. By practicing in this way right now, when you ascend to high spiritual paths, your experience will be like the verse,

One realizes (with wisdom) that all phenomena
  are like illusions,
And (with compassion) realizes that birth is like
  strolling into a park.
In times of prosperity and even in poverty,
One has no fear due to afflictions or adversity.

To relate this to the life of the Buddha, before he attained Awakening, he rejected the throne of a world ruler as if it were straw, and he lived by the Nairañjana River, unconcernedly applying himself to harsh austerities. This demonstrates that to experience the ambrosial meaning of your own existence, you must regard adversity and felicity as being of one taste.

Following his attainment of Awakening, the rulers of humans and gods up to the Akanishta heaven placed his feet upon their heads and honored him with all good things. The Brahmin Bharadhvaja abused him a hundred times; a haughty Brahmin's daughter accused him of sexual misconduct; and in the land of King Agnidatta he lived for three months on rotten horse fodder. On all such occasions he remained with an unfluctuating mind, like Mount Meru remaining unmoved by the wind. This demonstrates that to serve the needs of sentient beings, you must regard adversity and felicity as being of one taste.

Colophon

This teaching should be given by those with the life-style of the Kadampa masters, which is characterized by the saying, "When distressed, they do not complain. When happy, they are disillusioned." When it is taught by someone like myself, I feel as if my own tongue is embarrassed. Nevertheless, in order to accustom myself to regarding the eight mundane concerns (namely adversity and felicity, gain and loss, praise and blame, and good and bad reputation) as being of one taste, I, the old beggar Tenpe Nyima, have composed this in the Forest of Many Birds.

At the crest of the flourishing tree of publication,
May the flowers and fruits of this good counsel
Adorn the grove of the teachings of the Omni-
    scient One,
And may it bring delight to flocks of fortunate
    beings.

Subham astu sarvajagatam!
(May all the world be well!)

Part 2 *The Commentary*
by Venerable Gyatrul Rinpoche

Oral Commentary to the Root Text on the Transformation of Felicity and Adversity into the Spiritual Path

Here this evening, and any time when you are engaged in any aspect of dharma practice, you must first and foremost examine your motivation to see whether it is wholesome, unwholesome or indifferent. Whether you are listening to teachings, as you are here this evening, whether you are contemplating the meaning of the teachings that you've heard, or whether you are meditating or giving teachings, you must check carefully to see if the five mental afflictions[1] and the eight worldly concerns[2] are present in the mindstream. If so, you should uproot them because this would be an unwholesome intention, the cause for suffering and discontent.

Rather you should give rise to a wholesome intention which is to listen to the teachings, practice, or contemplate solely for the benefit of all parent sentient beings in order to accomplish their purpose. If you have no such motivation and remain indifferent with no real intention at all, then there will be no positive experience from the opportunity that you have at hand. Such an indifferent attitude bears no fruit. Since you need to produce something and that something should be as virtuous and positive as possible, it's extremely important that you give rise to a virtuous, wholesome intention.

The text that I am teaching from this evening is a very well-known text composed by the great mahasiddha and scholar Jigme Tenpe Nyima, the Third Dodrup Rinpoche, called *Transforming Felicity and Adversity into the Spiritual Path*.

According to the tradition, when teachings are received from a text such as this, initially one comes to understand the title of the text and the author's homage and personal aspiration. The aspiration will essentially state the author's commitment, or intention to accomplish by composing the text.

Considering the title *Transforming Felicity*, or happiness, *and Adversity*, suffering, *into the Spiritual Path*, for the great scholars of India and Tibet just to hear the title of a text, they will come to know everything that is contained within it. For those of mediocre sensibility, who nevertheless have some training, they will immediately come to understand whether this is going to be a teaching that falls under the category of sutra or tantra. For those beginners with basic scholastic training, when they hear or read the title, they will be able to determine some general idea of what the teaching will be about. This will also help them to be able to locate this text for future reference. Each text has its own title just like each of you have your own name.

Following the title, the author pays homage. In this case the author, Dodrup Tenpe Nyima, bows down to the noble Avalokiteshvara, the great Bodhisattva of Compassion. As he poetically writes, the reason this homage is rendered to Avalokiteshvara is because Avalokiteshvara is one who always rejoices at the happiness of others. As the Bodhisattva of Compassion, whenever the happiness of others is viewed – be it temporary or ultimate – he always rejoices. On the other hand, he is deeply saddened by the suffering of others. When he views all sentient beings of the six classes – those in the hell, hungry spirit, animal, human, titan and the deva realms – he realizes that they are somewhat like stubborn children.

Even though countless buddhas and great teachers have come in the past, live in the present, and will come in the future, still you have doubt. Still you are stubborn. Still you don't believe the teachings. Still you don't practice with open-hearted sincerity. It saddens Avalokiteshvara to see this predicament, yet he is one who has perfectly realized the qualities of great compassion. In doing so, he has released his own joy and sorrow. This means that, because he's exchanged himself for others and experiences only great compassion and has developed the qualities of that great compassion, he is self-liberated from this bondage of fluctuating joy and sorrow.

So it is Avalokiteshvara, whom you all are very aware of, who is the source of the one thousand buddhas of this light aeon – in fact the source of all buddhas and the emanation of the compassion of all buddhas. It is to such an embodiment that the author pays homage. By recalling the noble qualities and the virtues of Avalokiteshvara, he begins his commitment, which is to comprehensively explain in part the quintessential teachings on how to transform felicity and adversity into the spiritual path. This teaching is in fact considered to be the indispensable tool that all of the lamas of the past have relied upon. Without this tool they would be hard pressed to really accomplish the path because it is indeed the tool of those who are truly realized. It is considered to be invaluable in the world. It is like a wish-fulfilling jewel. It is indispensable and, once acquired, always needs to be maintained upon the path.

Considering then that this quintessential teaching is such a tool to use on the path, through this you will be able to accomplish your own purpose and the purpose of others which you have not yet been able to accomplish. This is something that you definitely need. It is just like a crucial little key to the path. The author commits himself to it by stating here in the text that he shall bring forth this explanation in two parts.

Transforming Adversity

The first part is the teaching on how to transform adversity into the spiritual path, and the second is the teaching on how to transform felicity into the spiritual path. We'll begin with the first section: the transformation of adversity. This explanation is given according to relative and ultimate truth.

It should be understood that, if someone is not on the spiritual path, then in a sense this teaching is irrelevant and somewhat useless. This teaching is meant for someone who is really practicing. Not only is it meant for such people, but also it is extremely important and indispensable as a tool to use throughout the many experiences on the path.

Whenever you are afflicted by another being or by anything at all, if you habituate your mind to dwelling on suffering only, then even the most insignificant, tiny circumstance will bring forth great distress. This occurs because you always want to accomplish your own needs and fulfill your own desires, which are primarily the eight worldly concerns, leading to non-virtue. This is your habituation. Since your mind is habituated to dwelling on negativity, if some small thing happens, some small affliction, then you immediately grasp onto this, shaping it into something very, very big. Even though initially it's something very insignificant, you allow it to bring you a huge amount of distress.

The example of relationships between men and women is convenient and perhaps the most obvious or pertinent example. When you meet someone that you are very attracted to, initially sparks fly between you that are so intense that you're satisfied by the mere sight of each other. Sometimes you don't even need to touch hands. But then, after your habitual nature begins to emerge (in reference to the first line of the text), since your mind is habituated to dwelling on suffering due to your attraction to non-virtue, then after even a very short time, the smallest condition will cause you extreme agitation or irritation and distress since it involves your relationship with that object of your attraction. Then you will blame your cherished object of attraction for this distress, when in fact you have created it yourselves. You've created it because you yourselves are attracted to suffering.

This happens because, whatever attitude is being cultivated towards happiness or adversity, by nature it will grow stronger. This is something that you become accustomed to.

For instance, most habits are considered to be somewhat harmful. Perhaps you like to eat hot chili, because you have cultivated an attitude to partake of hot chili. But in fact it burns your tongue; it makes you sweat; it burns holes in your stomach; and on and on. Nevertheless, it is your habit, so you keep eating it. Perhaps you like to drink liquor or have another habit such as this, which may actually be shortening your life, but in fact you keep on partaking of it, all the while knowing that it's really harming you. Because you are so attracted to it, you think it's something good.

Another example is bearing children. In this country this might not pertain as much as it did in Tibet, because here you have good hospitals where women go to give birth, which seems to be something that's carried out quite easily. But in Tibet there would be no place to go, and oftentimes the mother would lose her life. It was something quite dangerous and difficult. Yet after having one child, two, or three, they would keep on having more; four, five, so forth, all the while knowing the difficulty and suffering that must be endured.

The desire is stronger than knowing what the result will be, which is suffering. Because the habit or desire is so strong, the suffering is not considered to be so great.

In Tibet the men were all so macho that they would love to fight with each other and stick each other with swords, practically killing one another, just to have a little fun. They would come out of such a battle bruised, bleeding and sometimes near to their death, claiming, "Oh, I'm just fine. There's no problem." They wouldn't think that they were suffering because it was so important to them to maintain their status as a "real man."

This is what is meant by the idea of having habituated your mind. The strength of the mind can never be underestimated; it is the single most powerful force in existence. Any habituation will continue to increase, depending upon which direction it is headed. Eventually everything will lead to that.

Keeping this in mind, as the gradual habituation increases in the case of suffering, virtually everything that appears will eventually lead to misery. Even the most insignificant event will be the cause for much greater misery. Eventually there will be no possibility for happiness at all. This is something important to bear in mind in terms of your close relationships and family situations.

If you don't recognize that this is due to your own mental habits, you will blame it on external circumstances. Eventually the flames of hatred, non-virtue, and suffering will spread on endlessly, because you continue to believe that the problem arises from external circumstances.

This experience is also referred to as "appearances arising as enemies." You are very aware of this. You know of people or you may be someone who is easily angered. Such a person who is easily angered will experience many immediate negative reactions over incidental events. It's almost as though it took no effort to invoke such a response. The reason is their habituation. This is the habit of their mind, and they have failed to realize that they themselves have created this result. When the result itself gets so strong, it becomes harder and harder for them to realize the cause, because appearances are already arising as the enemy. They become bewildered because they feel the phenomena are outside of themselves. This is why they keep on reacting to external conditions and circumstances. Now anger, you should remember, is the leading cause for rebirth in the lowest realms.

Particularly in these degenerate times, sentient beings have a very weak power of discriminating awareness. Having failed to realize their primordial wisdom awareness nature, they confuse it for desire. Discriminating wisdom remains undeveloped. Therefore, there is weakness in mindfulness and mental alertness. They are not able to accurately pinpoint the accumulation of non-virtue and/or virtue, to successfully reject and accept. Most of the suffering that you are afflicted by in this corrupt era of difficult times really arises from your inferior powers of discrimination. Keeping that in mind, you should work harder to develop more wisdom. You say, "Watch your step." But you should watch before stepping. Watch and then step.

In particular if you are a dharma practitioner, the meaning of not being afflicted by the hindrances that arise from enemies, illness, malevolent spirits or anything else is not that you are actually going to be able to prevent the arising of such things in the future. In fact, killing one enemy will not guarantee you that a second one is not going to manifest. Or by freeing yourself from one illness, you cannot be guaranteed in cyclic existence that you are not going to acquire a new one. What this does mean, rather, is that hindrances are not able to arise as obstacles to the spiritual path. You do not and cannot avert them completely, but they do cease to hinder progress on the path because they become part of the path.

In order for this to happen, there are two things that you have to practice. The first is to dispense with the attitude of utter aversion to adversity. This you must eliminate. The second is to develop the attitude of good cheer in the face of adversity.

Let's begin with the first, which is dispensing with the attitude of utter aversion to adversity. There is really no reason to dislike adversity. Instead you must recognize again and again the pointlessness and the great detriment that arises from all of the miserable anxiety that is experienced through regarding adversity as something so totally unfavorable. If you keep reminding yourself how pointless this is, you will begin to realize this.

Then by trying to accustom yourself to the powerful anticipation of feeling "from now on whatever kind of adversity or suffering arises, I will not fear it; I will not befriend it; I will just allow it to be...," in this way great courage is cultivated in the face of adversity. This is no simple matter. But if you do this a number of times, then power develops and eventually the old habitual tendencies are put to rest.

If someone is always bickering with you, irritating

you, or causing an on-going negative relationship, after a while you may decide, "Well, I'm not going to dread this, because it's pointless; I'm going to just let it be." Rather than reacting, allow it to occur and observe it. After a while that individual who's always bickering and carrying on will either become too tired to continue or too embarrassed. If they are a decent individual, they will become embarrassed. If the individual is not so decent, they will simply become bored or tired.

The main point here is that the entire conflict is baseless. There's no need to continue developing something that has no point.

If you are in a house and there really are no ghosts or malevolent spirits there and yet you think there are and become quite paranoid about it, then every time the door slams shut or some wind comes through the room, your fear will be verified. This will intensify until actual ghosts are generated. The home will then become haunted; and then you will have developed a big problem.

In further developing your attitude of dispensing with this utter aversion to adversity, as the famed Shantideva said, "If suffering can be corrected, then there's no need to be despondent. And if it cannot be remedied, there is no benefit even if one becomes unhappy." This should be kept in mind since it clearly points out the uselessness of aversion to adversity.

While developing this attitude, you should maintain awareness of the great detriment of such aversion. If one does not react with strong anxiety and the mind is filled with courage and strength, it's easy to experience any difficulty. That so-called difficulty will become as flimsy as a light piece of cotton. Such was the experience of the Karmapa, whom many of you know since he passed away here in your own country. At the time of his passing, he was afflicted with so many different illnesses that were devouring his body. In the face of such hardship, even a rock would be hard pressed to remain patient. Yet each morning, as the doctor came in and asked him how he was, he said he was fine and was only concerned about how others were feeling. Here is a supreme example of someone who truly realized this practice. There are many, many true accounts about the great lamas who have realized the path of transforming adversity into the path. For example, H.H. the Dalai Lama, who lost his country and in spite of all the difficulties that he's had to undergo in his lifetime, has never spoken negatively about the Communist Chinese. When Mao Tse Tung died, His Holiness felt very sad, and he offered many prayers on his behalf. He considers all of these people to be objects of compassion and love. He has realized the pointlessness and the great detriment of such aversion. Chogyam Trungpa Rinpoche was another great example of one who underwent tremendous difficulties solely for the purpose of others.

The problem is, when you cherish yourself, you accomplish nothing. Is there a point to accomplishing nothing? If you really view it in this way, it is clear. The realized beings have exchanged self for others and cherish only others. They are now liberated, and you are not. There's a big difference.

If you fail to have this strength of mind whereby great adversity becomes as easy to handle as a light piece of cotton, due to your reacting with tremendous anxiety, you will become overwhelmingly oppressed with misery, even in the face of something very irrelevant.

For instance, because of the depth of true bodhicitta that the great bodhisattvas of the past had developed, many of them were actually able to offer parts of their bodies such as fingers, toes, or limbs. They had no pain in this experience because of the purity and strength of their mind. Instead of pain, they actually would experience gratitude and bliss.

While you are thinking of an attractive man or a gorgeous woman, even if you try to stop the desire that you have for this person, you will just wear yourself out. Right? Similarly, if you engross yourself in the miserable aspects of your adverse situation, then you will be unable to develop any sense of fortitude. It's something that will not be possible because of your focus.

This is why, as you know from the instructions that you have received in the past on guarding the doors of the senses, in the event of adversity, rather than becoming engrossed in its characteristics, you should get used to the recollection of the instructions that you have received. Place your mind in the natural state where the true nature is appreciated.

If you are confronted with an object of desire, then according to the vinaya, there are many ways to meditate upon that object as being repulsive. If it is someone's body, you may focus upon it as a heap of aggregates or something unclean by mentally dissecting the body into organs and parts. According to the mahayana, the method is to imagine its true nature to be illusory and to view it as an apparition – and to view oneself as an apparition as well. Another method is to view it as an object of compassion rather than as an object of desire. You may also consider the teachings in the preliminary practices[3] about how all living beings have at one time or another been your father or mother and have been kind to you, just like your father and mother of this life. Giving rise to immeasurable equanimity, you would then give rise to immeasurable compassion, which is much more sublime than attachment. Attachment only brings about its opposite, aversion.

If you are practicing vajrayana, then you will visualize the object as the deity and view the form as an expression of primordial awareness. It then becomes an object of devotion rather than an object of desire.

The second part of this teaching is to develop a sense of good cheer in the face of adversity. The cultivation of good cheer is a forthright attitude that regards adversity as an aid on the spiritual path. This is an experience of training. Whenever there is suffering, you will use it as an aid to the development of virtue. This is done by considering the benefits of virtue, the nature of cyclic existence to be that of suffering, and the unfailing truth of the law of cause and effect. No matter what kind of adversity arises, if you are lacking individual practices to apply to each case in accordance with your own mental abilities, then you may simply think, "If I am skillful, it is possible to achieve some real benefit as a result of this adversity." That may also be just theoretical, which is like saying that the goal is farther than the sky is from the earth.

Your hands must not be empty. It's not enough to just think, "Well there are these methods to be applied," because this is like the example given. You must have the individual practices to apply to each instance. For example, in order to really practice the six perfections, you have to receive teachings on how each perfection is developed in dependence upon an object, circumstance, and application of awareness. Let's consider the perfection of patience. Patience cannot be developed if there is no object through which patience can be cultivated. It is the same for morality, diligence, generosity and concentration. Wisdom is the awareness of the actual nature of subject, object, and activity as well as the skillful application of the method coupled with discriminating awareness.

In dependence upon suffering, you are able to accumulate the merit that is necessary to produce permanent happiness and liberation. If you examine the life stories and examples of the past saints and mahasiddhas, as well as the Jataka accounts of previous lives of Buddha Shakyamuni, you can clearly see how true practitioners dedicated their lives toward this pursuit – such as the example of Lord Buddha's past life when he was in Nepal and offered his body to the dying tigress and her cubs at the spot called "Namo Buddha."

First you must train. It's like getting ready to go into combat. The army has to train from the very first day in order to know how to handle the actual moment of combat. You are practitioners on the path; and, as spiritual warriors, you are preparing for your time of death. If you get these methods down now, then the transition will be something you can easily face. You will be well prepared.

There are some who use adversity as the support for training in the development of renunciation. This is done by recognizing that, as long as you wander without any self-control in cyclic existence, the occurrence of this type of adversity is not an injustice that's being imposed upon you. It's not something that is unfair. Rather, it is the play of the very nature of cyclic existence itself. Furthermore, while you are basically happy with this precious human rebirth, if it is difficult for you to bear such minor adversity now when you are in what is considered to be a fortunate rebirth, just imagine how very difficult it will be for you to endure the suffering of the lower realms. What would it be like if one were reborn in the lower realms where the suffering is truly unbearable?

Notice then that, if you are not able to be patient or to endure the small distress and misery that occurs now, you will not be able to endure it in the lower realms. Right now is the time to make sure that you do not have to endure the suffering of the lower realms.

Now is the time to realize that, until now, you have not been able to get out of this predicament without a true guide. This is why you are still wandering. The source of refuge, or guide needed, must have the full potency of having realized this predicament and passed through it successfully to reach the other side, the shore of liberation. When you choose your object of refuge, and go for refuge, you should be sure that you're taking refuge in someone who clearly sees the predicament of samsara, having been through it, and who knows precisely how to be set free from it. Such an experienced individual – a compassionate guide, a worthy guide, a guide who has the full qualifications – can guide you in the methods to be able to lead all other sentient beings out of cyclic existence.

Regarding the subject of transforming adversity into the path, one of the great ways that you suffer as practitioners is at the death of your spiritual mentors. This is because there is nothing more precious than your spiritual guides. When their physical presence leaves this world, you suffer tremendously. Yet the moment that the teacher departs from his or her corporeal form is also the moment that the teacher's mind mingles with the ultimate nature of truth. If, through your prayers, you can make a connection with this nature, there can be no greater benefit than that. At the time of the passing into nirvana of a highly realized being and in the days that follow, your suffering can turn to very strong development of realization on the path, once again due to the teacher's kindness.

Developing a sense of good cheer in the face of adversity, you can specifically use adversity as the support for refuge and true spiritual development. I am discussing how you relate to your suffering, how you relate to your adversity, as it affects you in life and on the path. Now, as you know, whenever you are suffering by way of the body, speech, and mind, be it physical illness or a mental affliction (which seems to be the affliction of malevolent spirits, obstructive forces, or external enemies), this is a very big deal to you. Usually it appears as something major. Even if it's minor, you make it into some great distress. If you lose a little money or if someone speaks nastily to you, it invokes a strong reaction. This is called "appearances arising as the enemy."

When your habituation to adversity reaches such a point that you actually fall prey to appearances arising as the enemy, it means that you no longer have patience for suffering. This presents the same problem mentioned earlier. If you can't bear the minor aspects of adversity in this, the best rebirth in cyclic existence, the precious human rebirth, what will you do when you're reborn in the three lower realms? Samsara is so vast, so deep and limitless, and the number of sentient beings within samsara are equal to that. All of them want to be free; all of them desire liberation. You should consider then how unnecessary or pointless it is to think that your small problems in this fortunate life are so great, when in fact they really are not.

Any rebirth in this ocean of cyclic existence will by nature bring this type of discontent or suffering. Since you've been in this cycle of rebirths from beginningless time until now and you are still not free, it points out the fact that help is needed. Refuge is necessary. Adversity then becomes the support for training in refuge, which demonstrates that adversity is used to your advantage.

Taking refuge in a supreme object is not to become overpowered or controlled by someone or something. It is so one can be assisted to reach liberation, freedom from the ocean of suffering. It's for your own security. It's for your own benefit. It really has nothing to do with the object of your refuge or benefiting the object. Your object of refuge should be unmistaken. In this case the supreme object of refuge is Lord Buddha Shakyamuni as the one who is able to accomplish the purpose of all beings, having fully accomplished his own self-interest. In Buddhism, when refuge is taken in the Three Jewels, there are different ways of taking and understanding refuge according to the different sensibilities of the aspirants. Some individuals will be led to relate to refuge externally. Some will be led to understand externally and internally, some secretly, some extremely secretly. In both sutra and tantra, the outer, external refuge in the Three Jewels – Buddha, Dharma and Sangha – is fully embraced.

The inner manner of embracing refuge is practiced specifically in tantra by those who are practicing the generation stage. This is the transformation of the buddha, dharma and sangha into the lama, yidam and dakini. The lama is the spiritual guide; the yidam is the meditation deity; and the dakini represents the female principle of enlightened awareness. Those who are practicing completion stage transform the inner into the secret refuge taken in the channels, energies, and essential fluids. The channels are understood to be the nirmanakaya; the energies are understood to be the sambhogakaya; and the essential fluid is the dharmakaya. For those who join the two stages indivisibly to practice the extremely secret approach, refuge is taken directly in the nature of the mind: the essence, the nature, and the unobstructed quality of compassion. This refers to the intrinsic awareness nature of mind whereby the object, the subject, and the activity arise simultaneously and samsara and nirvana are experienced as one flavor. Understanding this is dependent upon the level of individual development. This is not something that can be grasped without having already achieved or developed your noble qualities to a certain state of awareness.

When you practice going for refuge and train in refuge as a support for practice, you must have the mental conviction that considers that whatever happens, you shall entrust yourself to the Three Jewels alone and never abandon them under *any* circumstances, even if it must cost you your own life. This type of refuge is not being filled with faith and devotion for a few days or for a short period of time. This is something that goes far beyond that. This is more important than your own life. Your own life is still temporary. It's short lived. After that, then what?

The next step is using adversity as the support for dispelling arrogance. Understand that arrogance, pride, or haughtiness is a very potent mental affliction with the potential to destroy everything wholesome and all of one's efforts towards liberation. Here, in using adversity as the support for dispelling arrogance specifically, bear in mind the way in which you lack self control and the way in which you continuously fail to escape being controlled by your own adversity. Therefore, recognizing that failure of yours also has the potency to snuff out any pride you might have had about yourselves as practitioners.

Pride is something that is very nasty and sneaky because, without your even noticing it, it actually closes the door to the development of pure qualities. If you think you already know something, then even while you're listening to teachings or contemplating teachings, you already have an attitude that you know something more than that. This prevents you from learning about what you are hearing. When you achieve the status of full awakening and are free from the bondage of cyclic existence, then you can have some sense of true confidence that you know something because your mind is finally free from mental darkness.

There is, however, a kind of pride that is necessary – deity pride. This is not the same as ordinary pride. When you practice vajrayana and generate self-nature as the deity, you become aware of your primordial wisdom nature and its expression or embodiment as a particular deity – peaceful, wrathful, or whatever class the deity belongs to. This expression arises in order to tame the minds of sentient beings as well as your own mind. While you are in that state of pure awareness, you are awakening the seed which leads to liberation. On the other hand, ordinary pride produces the seed of discontent and suffering, because it is a mental affliction. There is a big difference here which should be recognized.

Those who suffer from the mental affliction of pride always want to put others below them. They maintain an attitude of being more supreme than others – perhaps the best in the world. With a prideful mind, you will always think that you are right. This prevents you from learning anything, because you always feel that your way is the best.

The next step is to use adversity as the support for purifying unwholesome actions or negative karmic accumulations. In this case you consider that such adversity as this as well as all of the greater adversities arise only as a result of negative causes. Here you should consider the four points about karma: that actions invariably give rise to corresponding effects, that the effects of actions increase, that one never experiences the effects of actions that were not committed, and finally that deeds committed never fail to produce results. Since this is the unfailing law of karma, you need to carefully consider all of your negative karmic accumulations. All negative accumulations are caused because of your futile attempts to bring some benefit to this cherished self of yours. From that you are just planting the seeds for whatever result will ripen. Whether great or small, it just depends on the motivation behind the cause, but surely that result will be experienced.

Please bear in mind then that, if you don't want adversity, you should avoid its cause, non-virtue. Why continue to produce the cause of negative karma when you don't want that result? This is what you should consider. Then consider that, by means of the four remedial powers, you should disclose such actions that you've already amassed and strive to restrain from accumulating them again in the future. Now most of you are familiar with the four remedial powers, which are the backbone of the Vajrasattva purification practice. To be free from negative causes, you must apply these four powers through Vajrasattva purification and recitation. This points out that non-virtue has a quality – it is impermanent and can be removed. It can be fully purified.

These four powers are effective only if they are complete. They are the power of the support, visualizing Vajrasattva above the crown of one's head; the power of remorse, recollection of one's past misdeeds, shortcomings, and negative accumulations;

the power of the purification, the descent of the nectar from Vajrasattva's head down into your crown and body, purifying negative accumulations; and finally the power of the vow not to repeat these negativities in the future. The final power to never repeat the negativity again is probably the most important. These days there are many prisoners who get put into jail who then confess and promise to never repeat their crime. Then they're let out on parole, and they repeat their crime. If you just continue to produce the same negative causes although you've purified them, no one can promise a clear karmic slate. This is totally dependent upon the power of your own commitment.

You are very familiar with this condition, or habituation of repeating your faults, especially amongst your loved ones within the family circle. The husband, the male, may be cheating on his partner, his wife or the woman whom he is living with or has a commitment to, and she finds out about it, then he promises, "Oh, I'll never do it again. I promise, I promise." So for a few days there's happiness between them, and everything's fine. Then after a little while, that old habit re-emerges, and the problem occurs again. This leads to divorce, and then later on to another marriage. Then it happens again. This is a cycle you are very familiar with.

The next step is to use adversity as a support for attracting one to virtue or wholesome deeds. That's done by pondering at length that, if you take some delight in happiness which is the opposite of adversity or unhappiness, then you should strive for its cause which is virtue. What is virtue? From the point of view of the explanation of the ten root non-virtues, virtue is the opposite of those ten. It's not just the avoidance of killing, stealing, adultery, lying, slander, harsh speech, idle gossip, craving, ill will, and wrong view; it is to intentionally practice the opposite of those ten. It's not enough just to be attracted to virtue. One has to practice virtue and strive for its cause in various ways, however one can, to progress in the direction of virtue. Being attracted to virtue is somewhat like the first aspect of bodhicitta, which is aspirational. Aspirational bodhicitta is the development of the four immeasurables (love, compassion, joy, and equanimity). Actually striving to accomplish virtue, to put that attraction into one's practice or into one's mainstream of activities is practical bodhicitta, the second aspect of bodhicitta. Here you strive to engage in the practice of the six perfections (generosity, morality, patience, perseverance, concentration, and wisdom).

If someone asks you, "Do you like happiness?" of course you will answer, "Yes." Happiness is the result of virtuous wholesome causes. To have an attitude such as, "I like it but I can't really create it. Why? Because I'm too lazy or I'm not motivated," or all the many different excuses that you come up with, then what's the point of just liking it? How far will that get you? To be attracted to virtue is not enough. It must be developed by way of body, speech, and mind through cultivating the wisdoms of hearing, contemplating, and meditation.

The next step is to use adversity as the support for training in compassion. Here you reflect on the many ways in which other sentient beings just like yourself are afflicted with suffering which is for the most part far greater than your own. It is important to train yourself in the contemplation upon the futility of cyclic existence and the way in which all sentient beings are lost in samsara as the result of what they've caused, contradicting their own wishes. Especially try to visualize the three lower realms of existence and how unbearable the suffering in those realms must be. Try to bring out the wish that all beings may be freed from their suffering and pray for them until you feel you cannot bear it until all beings are freed.

The reason that immeasurable impartiality must be developed first is so that one realizes the equality of all living beings. After that, one follows the corresponding training to develop immeasurable love, compassion, and joy.

Next, adversity is used as the support for cultivating the attitude of cherishing others more than oneself. Here you should consider that the reason that you're not free from such adversity is that you've always been self-centered. Now rather than that, you should vow to dedicate yourself to cherishing others by clearly understanding this to be the source of happiness and the source of prosperity. You have to consider that, because of your self-centeredness which causes you to fluctuate between attachment, aversion, and indifference, you have created this problem of adversity. Realizing this to be the main root of the problem now, you are clear that you must exchange that self-cherishing for the cherishing of others.

This is what all the buddhas and bodhisattvas have realized and put into practice. Simply put, they realized this problem, exchanged self for others, and became liberated. You, on the other hand, have not done that. That's the difference between those of you who are still sentient beings and those who are liberated and are called buddhas and bodhisattvas. You cherish yourselves more than others. They cherish others more than themselves.

This is something that you have to train in because your habit of being self-centered is so strong. In meditation the mind is trained to become accustomed to the exchange of self for others. If you think that you can easily accomplish this, you might be disappointed when some strong adversity arises and you react immediately. Please do not consider that this habit is going to subside very easily. Training is a slow process. You shouldn't have expectations that are too high or you will experience low ebbs of disappointment.

In Tibet there was one Geshe who was meditating on patience. That was his main practice. So he meditated and meditated all the time. Whenever a student would come and say, "Teacher, Geshe-la, what are you meditating upon?" he would always reply, "Patience." So different students would come and again ask the same question, "What are you meditating upon?" "Patience." One time one student came along and said, "Oh teacher, what are you meditating upon?" And he replied, "Patience." Then the student said, "Eat shit." And Geshe-la replied, "What?! What are you talking about? You eat shit."

It's very easy for you to be wholesome and virtuous and spiritual when things are going right. But as soon as a little bit of adversity arises, then the real test begins. That's the time when you can find out how well your practice has been proceeding, especially when you look at how you deal with your family life. There's a good way to test yourselves.

When you are experiencing tremendous misfortune that seems to be staring you in the face, this indicates the onset of difficult times. You all have experienced this. That's the very time that it is crucial to be familiar with these practices by having previously accomplished the training. This is why you train. You should place your emphasis on the most vivid experience, knowing where your weaknesses are.

Furthermore, it's not really enough for adversity just to become an aid to your spiritual practice. This is still a beginning step. It is a vital point that you should cultivate a continuous sense of joy or gratitude as a result of recognizing that this is happening. Adversity as an aid to your spiritual practice is something to truly rejoice over.

There are some other problems that may arise from this point which I would like to bring out. Many Tibetans actually get involved on the spiritual path, take ordination, join monasteries or scholastic colleges or practice colleges, because they are able to find security and sponsorship in such institutions. It is safe there because they will receive food, clothing, and necessities. This allows for easy survival. It's difficult to survive as a refugee in India, Nepal and elsewhere. Even in Tibet this was the case. Many would enter monasteries to have a comfortable life where they'd be taken care of. A lot of Americans come to the path because they're lost, confused or overwhelmed. To escape from that predicament, they become Buddhists and enter the spiritual path.

In a sense this is what is meant by saying it's not enough for adversity to become an aid to your spiritual practice. In the worst sense, you can use adversity as an excuse for entering the path. The main point to bring out is that it is vital that you cultivate this strong and continuous sense of gratitude. It is through gratitude that even severe suffering will be extremely agreeable. This is how it is that practitioners achieve enlightenment in one body and in one lifetime. There's no other way, because they have the ultimate goal in mind. If you dwell only on the temporary hardships, which is where you get caught up and where you stop, how can you proceed? You must understand that temporary hardships are part of the path. This is what leads to the ultimate state of liberation. If you look at Milarepa, Longchenpa, all of the great masters of the past who are your examples, you can clearly determine that there's no other way. You must face up to this and develop this sense of good cheer and gratitude when you have temporary difficulties, knowing that they will change. They are a part of what leads all of you to ultimate bliss.

Suffering is very kind to you. If you don't have suffering, you will not turn from attraction to cyclic existence, which means you will never be free. It's as simple as that.

Sometimes it's very difficult to take a foul-tasting medicine, for instance Chinese medicinal tea. You take it because you know that it will benefit you. How difficult is it to undergo surgery, yet you know that there's a chance that your illness may be cured. Just like that, it's extremely difficult to accomplish dharma.

How could it be otherwise? Yet, if you understand that this suffering, although severe, is something agreeable to what your goal is and, in fact, can be endured quite easily by facing adversity with a sense of good cheer, your inability to endure physical pain will be overcome. Because one has a sense of mental well-being, which means mental strength, the mind becomes strong and begins to feel peaceful or happy about the practice. That alone makes the physical pain seem like something imperceptible. Then the inability for physical pain to afflict the mind is achieved. This is something that is a prerequisite for someone who is going to go deeper into dharma practice, particularly the ability to overcome illness by means of inner strength. This indicates that one is able to overcome physical pain through one's sense of mental well-being, suggesting that this is also the same way to overcome enemies, demonic force possession, and on and on.

What is also being brought out here is that reversing this attitude of aversion towards adversity is the basis for causing adversity to arise as the spiritual path. As long as your mind is still troubled with anxiety and despair, it's impossible for adversity to be brought onto the path. If the mind is troubled and you're trying to force yourself to endure suffering, that's not going to work. The only way that it will work is if you are able to consider the points of this training, to apply them to each experience, and to train gradually.

By performing the training according to the teachings, bringing adversity onto the path, you will encounter special benefits. During those experiences, you will see for yourself how it helps your spiritual path; and your sense of well-being will continue to increase. You will be inspired to continue on with this type of practice.

Initially you must practice with some minor adversity. That's a very important point. Gradually it will become easier, until finally you will be able to practice in the face of great adversity. You must never try to practice in the face of great adversity as a beginner.

As you develop each virtue on the path, it's just like developing patience. First, you learn to be patient with yourself. Once you've been able to see some effective positive results and unprecedented benefits, then you can practice patience with your spouse, family, friends, and so forth. Once you see benefits there, you can practice patience with other objects that are more difficult to practice with. Training in generosity may begin with something as simple as giving something from the right hand to the left hand and back to the right hand, then giving it to the hand of another, like your spouse or your child, and then to the hand of a friend, and eventually to the hand of a stranger. Like this, minor moves to major.

It is difficult for you to expect to be able to reach an experience that is beyond the capacity of your own mind, yet at the same time it's not a case where everyone is the same. Usually approaching the path, you begin with the essence of hinayana. Once this is realized, you move to the essence of mahayana. And once this is realized, you move to vajrayana. But there are those individuals who, by the power of their past prayers and aspirations, karmic causes and results, may go straight to vajrayana or to mahayana, who may not need to go through the graduated stages of development. People are on different levels. We all have different sensibilities and are all not going to be the same. You shouldn't try to categorize yourselves. You should check up on your own capacities and be instructed to train accordingly.

In between meditation sessions, you should make regular prayers to your spiritual teacher and to the Three Jewels so that adversity will arise as the spiritual path. When you've noticed that the power of your mind is beginning to increase, you should then make offerings to the Three Jewels and to the spiritual teacher as an expression of gratitude. When you are experiencing your own development of this transformation of adversity into the path, you should pray to your teacher and the Three Jewels to give you more unfavorable circumstances, so that your practice can deepen – like praying that you would be afflicted by spirits, ghosts or some horribly distracting situation.

We've been discussing in a deeper sense the kindness of adversity and obstacles. I have my own experience with my mother of this life who was a very good example for me. She was always preoccupied with negative habits. Later in her life she became blind. She used to say the vows of refuge on a regular basis, but otherwise her mind was preoccupied with worldly concerns. After I was taken from her, then her suffering increased. Later she began praying constantly to Chenrezig and reciting OM MANI PADME HUM. She was able to repeat several million recitations of the Mani mantra. Eventually before her death, her sight returned. Her white hair began turning black, and she even grew some new teeth in her mouth. There were some very amazing signs at the time of her death. I feel that, based on knowing her nature, if she hadn't become blind, this would never have happened.

Several of my friends or students have fallen ill with cancer and other incurable diseases. After receiving teachings on Vajrasattva practice, then they began to practice seriously. Some of them were able to be completely cured. Others, at the time of their death, were very happy to die and had no regrets at all, showing very good signs of accomplishment at that moment. Now I know for a fact because these were students and friends of mine that if they had not fallen ill, this would never have happened. It was due to the suffering of physical illness that they were brought to the path of practice.

Speaking for myself, in Tibet I had seven hundred monks in my own monastery before the Cultural Revolution. After I escaped in 1959, many of these monks were murdered, especially the high lamas. I am the only survivor from my monastery who escaped. After coming to India, I had the opportunity to meet the great realized beings of our time such as the Dalai Lama, the Karmapa, Dudjom Rinpoche, Kalu Rinpoche, and many others. If I hadn't left Tibet and undergone this difficult transition, I would still be there in some sort of high position in my monastery thinking of myself as being a great lama. In fact, this gave me the opportunity to meet the great lamas elsewhere and to go to the great power spots such as Bodhgaya, Sarnath, and many others.

The next point to consider is that, when you first begin to practice, it is helpful to meditate in an environment where you are removed from distractions. This advice is usually given to beginners. Ideally you retreat to an isolated place where you're not so easily distracted. This is because in the midst of distractions, it is easy to be diverted by unwholesome companions and others who influence you to stray from the direction that you've taken. On the other hand, there are those who choose to practice in isolated places like cemeteries in order to be among the gods and spirits.

All of the different distractions that arise are valid in that they tend to lead you from your course. You may worry about possessions, relatives, get caught up in some other bad habits, or get carried away by the distractions that other humans cause. On the other hand, if you go to a burial ground to practice, you can train in an environment where there are non-human spirits. If you can stabilize the mind in such an unruly environment, then your training will deepen, and the mind will become more peaceful.

Those who decide to practice in burial grounds may do so in order to train in the illusory nature of the manifestations of gods and demons. One attempts to eliminate the inner delusions through this method. There is a well-known account of a practitioner of chöd (exorcism of grasping to appearances). While he was in the burial ground practicing, deeply engrossed in his meditation, chant, and use of the ritual instruments, along came a thief who tried to steal his bag and some other possessions. While attempting to do so, the thief became very frightened. Overcome by fear, he took out his knife and sliced off the head of the practitioner while he was deeply absorbed in practice. When the head dropped off and hit the ground, the thief became horrified and ran far away. This chöd practitioner, who was deeply involved in the unity of appearances and emptiness, thought that this was just a false apparition manifesting as an obstacle. Without a second thought he just reached down, picked up his head and placed it back in position while he continued on with the practice. To him this was just part of the practice. When his meditation was complete, he put his instruments away and went back home.

A few days later, he was out circumambulating at the stupa nearby and the same thief saw him there and recognized him as the very yogin whose head he had sliced off. He was overcome with terror and remorse to see him there alive and well. If he hadn't said anything, it would have been just fine; but, unfortunately, he went up to the yogin, and prostrated himself, confessing what he had done. The yogin immediately got doubt about it and he said, "Oh, so you're the one who really came and cut off my head." With that thought, his head fell off and he died.

In Tibet there are so many examples that I have personally experienced with great lamas who have this level of advanced realization. If you don't ask them how they're feeling, they will never be sick. But if you go to them and say, "Oh, Rinpoche, how do you feel today?" then immediately they'll be bent over with pain. I have seen some great lamas burst out in tears as an expression of their pain, whereas if you hadn't brought the subject up, they were perfectly fine. It was very much like this with H.H. Dudjom Rinpoche. If you went in his presence and said, "Oh, Rinpoche, you must not be feeling very well," or

"How are you feeling today? Are you okay?" then he would say, "Oh, yes, I don't feel so well." Then he would begin to show signs of illness. But if you went to him and said, "Oh, Rinpoche, you must be feeling very well," he would say, "Oh, yes, I'm feeling fine." This demonstrates to you the power of discursive thoughts.

Whatever negative circumstance befalls you, be it a physical illness or some bad news, you have an opportunity to use this adversity as the very path itself. Right now you are all suffering from the bad news of the passing of H.H. Khyentse Rinpoche, but this is a time that you ought to apply this type of training. If there were nothing that you could do with bad news but suffer, then that would be one thing; but you now have all these methods through which to make the most of the opportunity. The time has come to employ the methods.

If at first something seems as though it may be harmful, if you can turn from aversion and open yourself to its potency to become the path, your strength on the path will surely increase. In order for all this to happen, you simply have to stop seeing circumstances as harmful situations or as something that is wrong. Give all your effort towards practicing to see it as something that is valuable. Based on that, you develop a sense of good cheer. Trying to practice this is the essence of the first aspect of the teaching on the transformation of adversity into the path.

This way of transforming mental afflictions into the path automatically transforms one's own manner. You will become gentle-minded, easygoing, and courageous. Furthermore, there will be no obstacles to your spiritual practice. They will disappear. All of the unfavorable circumstances will arise as something challenging and fortunate.

You can consider that, in order to follow the spiritual path in a degenerate era, this is the indispensable armor, the indispensable weapon, the indispensable key. It is the armor that has been worn by all of the great saints of the past. If you're free of the suffering of anxiety, other types of suffering and misery will drop away and vanish like soldiers who put down their weapons.

Those who are wise see that all experiences of adversity and felicity depend upon the mind. They seek happiness that arises from within the mind. They realize then that all the causes for happiness come from within themselves, and no longer need to be dependent upon external circumstances. They achieve what is called personal freedom or self-control. They're not afflicted by the harms of other sentient beings. If you have personal power or freedom, then this will be something that holds true even at the time of death. You are always free, because *you* are free.

Without accomplishing this, you are like the foolish whose minds never become steady. There will be an endless flood of obstacles that seem to be plaguing you which go on and on. The foolish then go running after external objects in their pursuit of happiness. Whatever happiness they achieve is something that leads to yet more suffering. There arises an inability to be satisfied because, whenever you think happiness arises due to external events, this will be endless. Such is the example of myself in having built a temple, and wanting to do retreat; the more elaborate it gets, the more elaborate it has to become. The time for a simple life and a simple retreat continues to slip farther away. Life gets more and more complicated rather than more and more simple.

This is a brief explanation of how to use adversity as the path. You may elaborate on this by using your preliminary practices as a support for this training. Then you can make use of many different contemplations to transform adversity and felicity. For example, using the six realms of existence while contemplating cyclic existence, or the four noble truths. Based on suffering, there's a cause; and based on the cause of suffering, the path arises. Based on the path, there's an end to suffering. Similarly you can apply this to the different contemplations and practices that you are already engaged in, including the Seven-Point Mind Training and the study of Shantideva's *Bodhicharyavatara*, the *Guide to a Bodhisattva's Way of Life*.

The second subdivision for this section on transforming adversity into the spiritual path is by means of ultimate truth. The discussion that we've just had is by means of relative truth. Concerning ultimate truth, one has to have the instrument of such reasoning as awareness of the four extreme views and the refutation of the four extreme views, so that the mind is able to ascertain emptiness. Abiding in the awareness of the nature of emptiness is the essence of the intrinsic awareness nature of the mind. In the essence of intrinsic awareness, the conceptual proliferations are automatically arrested. This occurs spontaneously without effort.

In this nature, which is the nature of truth, unfavorable circumstances and adversity as well as their names are not to be found; they are non-existent. Where did they go? They dissolved into the expanse of the view. They arose from the view; they dissolve in the view. Where is the view? Is it outside of yourself? Your nature is the view.

The view is to believe in and understand the buddha nature, the essence of all the buddhas. If one knows the buddha nature, then that is to know the unchanging essence which is free from any limitation, the original primordial nature of the mind as it is. This is not like a light bulb that suddenly comes on or something that is newly acquired. It is the nature as it has always been and always will be: primordially perfect. To recognize the buddha nature is the view. To fail to recognize the buddha nature is to deviate into confusion. If you recognize your buddha nature, this is the same as having an audience with all the buddhas. You will meet face to face with all your root teachers.

Where is it? How can you see it? Why don't you see it? You are in a state of obscurity which is only temporary, like a suddenly-arising condition such as the clouds that obscure the sun. You know the sun is there, as it always is; but you cannot see it, because it is temporarily covered by clouds. That does not mean the sun is no longer there. Like that, while you are in this sudden condition of habituation with karmic afflictions and obscurations, you must train on the path to remove them. The path is practiced only to remove obscurations and to accumulate merit, so that you can realize your own nature. When the wind comes along and blows the clouds away, the sun is then revealed. Such is the potency of the path through which the obscurations dissolve. The buddha nature is revealed.

Transforming Felicity

The second part of the teaching concerns transforming felicity into the spiritual path by means of relative truth and ultimate truth. Whenever you consider there is bliss and the objective conditions for bliss occur, if you fall under the control of that by becoming arrogant or conceited, then that will fester as an obstruction to the spiritual path. Rather than thinking about what has caused this happiness, which most probably is the accumulation of merit or the removal of obscurations, as soon as the bliss occurs, you think, "That's my nature." Based on that, you become arrogant or lazy, thinking, "Well, I've accomplished it." This is the greatest obstacle to the spiritual path. This is what creates the realms of deva-gods. Oftentimes it is said that people can handle only a little bit of felicity, but they can handle a lot of adversity. This is because happiness on the spiritual path is the most difficult thing to handle. Once it arises, that's where the path stops.

In order not to deviate in this way, the crucial point is that you should regard all of these states of happiness and these conditions of bliss as being impermanent and unsatisfactory. You should also develop a strong sense of disillusionment towards them by realizing that they have no essence. Directing your mind in this way is quite useful. Thinking that the pleasures of the world are trifling, that even the relationships and strong attractions between men and women, attraction to status, fame, and glory are all impermanent gives rise to a sense of disillusionment with all of this. Realize that all of you are impermanent and every aspect of your life's experience must be impermanent also.

This does not mean that it is necessary to give it all up. Giving up happiness is not the practice. The main point is not to become mesmerized by happiness as the end result. You realize that, "Ah, now, the good quality of this is that I am fortunate, and this is another result of the great fortune of the path and the result of the accumulation of merit and wholesome deeds. Even more than ever, I will carry on with the work at hand to achieve liberation from cyclic existence." So with more diligence and more courage, you continue listening to teachings, contemplating, meditating, and appreciating this precious human rebirth. One realizes that in fact, "I have an opportunity here to make offerings. I can practice. I can accomplish the purpose of self and others."

Thinking that the opportunity to practice dharma in such a state of happiness is one's great fortune is extremely useful. If freedom is impaired by suffering, then it's difficult to attain enlightenment. Furthermore, if you consider that if you convert all of your happiness into dharma and that dharma itself is the source of happiness, happiness and dharma are totally conducive. They're complementary. By joining the two together, the result will be a constant connection with dharma in all of your future lifetimes.

This point is usually lost because, once happiness occurs, you are not satisfied, thinking you need more. You think that your situation can improve so you keep on trying to improve it until you are hopelessly entangled once again.

It is necessary to recognize the agreeable as something that's agreeable and to try to devote oneself to realizing what it is to be satisfied and content. Other practices that bring felicity into the path include contemplating the kindness of the Three Jewels of refuge, and the instructions for cultivating the spirit of awakening. There are many, many other ways; however, these methods alone are more than sufficient.

When practicing in solitude, the same advice applies as for transforming adversity into the path. Apply this training and alternately practice to accumulate merit and purify negative karma.

Concerning the transformation of felicity into the spiritual path by means of ultimate truth, it is exactly the same as the transformation of adversity by means of ultimate truth. In the nature of truth, there is no distinction between good and bad, better or worse.

When you are happy like you are now, with the freedom to practice dharma, if you postpone the practice, then in the future when you become seriously ill or approach your death, at that time you will not have the power to practice. It is most important to cultivate that power to practice while you are able and happy. If you do not practice when you're happy, then when will you practice?

It is important to consider that, now while you do have this state of tremendous freedom, your conditions are ripe with opportunity. It is inconceivable when you really consider just how fortunate you are. In order to avoid wasting this opportunity and the intense regret that arises at the moment of death, this present opportunity must be seized. Realize that dharma practice is something that accumulates gradually, like tiny little drops. Eventually there is the potential to become a large body of water. Virtue is accumulated just like that. All the virtue that you've accumulated in the past is still with you; it will never leave you. The more and more that you accumulate it, the stronger and stronger it becomes. However, you must remember that it's never exhausted if you generate the pure motivation prior to every practice and dedicate the merit at the end. You must always have a pure motivation in the beginning, then a pure awareness of the practice, and dedication at the end. Practice is not just only formal sitting or contemplating. Practice must be carried into all aspects of daily life with the bodhicitta attitude of loving-kindness and compassion. If you are experiencing negative thoughts or harmful intentions, this is the play of the mental afflictions of the five poisons. You must always check throughout your daily experience to make sure that the mind is motivated by goodness.

If you think about some of the real problems that you face, it seems that you are easily influenced by external conditions. If you lose something, you become very upset. If you lose one of your important possessions or if someone speaks unkindly to you, it hurts you deeply. It's very easy for you to react. In one instant, one state of mind can change to another just based on one word, sign, or action. On the other hand, if something good occurs – perhaps you receive a compliment from someone – it brings a surge of pleasure. This can produce a total change from unhappiness to happiness instantaneously due to ego gratification. I believe that this is the main obstacle to progress on the path, because the emphasis on what is important is mistaken.

For the most part the things that you focus on in life as important are really not important at all. That is proven by the way that you react and relate. The mind has the strongest reaction to meaningless things and the weakest reaction to the most important things, in particular the precious human rebirth. Every second of every day this chance slips away since life gets shorter, not longer. There is only one vessel through which enlightenment can be reached; the precious human rebirth is the only vessel through which one achieves liberation in one body and in one lifetime. Furthermore, you have met with the most profound aspect of the Buddha's teachings and have connections with great lamas who have been extremely kind. The thought of losing all of that should be very upsetting. When a prized possession is lost, it is very upsetting. The point is that the emphasis is off balance. This needs to be examined and readjusted.

I want to conclude by reminding everyone that, since you've all received many empowerments, transmissions, and teachings, you must always take care to keep your samaya pure and to maintain your place of practice with pure samaya. It's very good if you always have a chance to meditate in this kind of conducive environment. However, if you don't have a chance to do retreat or actually sit in formal meditation, you don't need to feel disheartened. You can always practice while going about your daily routine and even while driving. Every time you get into the car, that can be the time that you recite the Vajrasattva mantra, for instance. So that becomes your driving retreat. You can use each part of your day like this. You don't have to feel that you need to have a special time for practice, because it's difficult to have "special time." If you wait for special time, you might wait a long time. That's my own experience.

You should always try to serve and repay the kindness of your spiritual teachers. When the lamas leave this world, going to their body and crying is not the way to please them. The way to please them is to work for the welfare of sentient beings and to honor and uphold their teachings. You must serve and dedicate your life to others, whether you think you're qualified or not. Just do your best. That's the greatest offering, the greatest rendering of praise, and the greatest way to fulfill the kindness that they've shown to you.

Part II
DREAM YOGA

Releasing Oneself from Essential Delusion
Notes on the Written Instruction in the
Vajrasattva Mind Accomplishment of Dreams
by
Lochen Dharma Shri

Translated by
B. Alan Wallace

Commentary by
Venerable Gyatrul Rinpoche

Translated by
Sangye Khandro

Part 1   The Root Text
by Lochen Dharma Shri

Releasing Oneself from Essential Delusion
Notes on the Written Instruction in the Vajrasattva Mind Accomplishment of Dreams

Om Svasti!

By setting free the apprehender and the apprehended in the expanse of self-awareness,
The immutable energy-mind of clear light (is
revealed) as the illusory deity.
Offering homage to the guide and spiritual mentor Vajrasattva,
I shall reveal the quintessential instruction on
apprehending and transforming dreams.

In the brief instruction on the phases of the Vajrasattva Mind Accomplishment, there are two parts –

preparation and actual practice – with respect to putting into practice the quintessential teachings on dreams.

THE PREPARATION

First purify your mindstream with the preliminary practices.

At the outset, repeatedly reflect on the difficulty of obtaining this life of endowment and leisure. Cultivate awareness of impermanence by thinking, "Now I have obtained such a life; but I shall certainly die, and there is no certainty when death will occur." Recognize that no matter where you are born in the cycle of existence, in a high or low state, everything entails involvement in dissatisfaction. Thus, seeing that all is pointless, restrain your mind with a powerful sense of disillusionment.

Imagine your dwelling to be as a pure realm, and in the space in front of you visualize on a high and broad throne your spiritual mentor in the form of Vajrasattva, in the nature of all the combined objects of refuge. Thinking, "If I and all other sentient beings, fearing the misery of the cycle of existence, seek refuge, the holy spiritual mentor knows," go for refuge. Recognizing all sentient beings throughout space as your own kindly parents, arouse your heart with overwhelming compassion. Generate the spirit of awakening by thinking, "I shall liberate all sentient beings from suffering and bring them to the attainment of perfect awakening. To do so, I shall meditate on the profound path."

At the crown of your head, meditate on your spiritual mentor in the nature of all the combined objects of refuge, and with reverence that makes your hair stand on end and brings tears to your eyes, earnestly pray that you apprehend your dreams and transform them through training. Finally, imagine your spiritual mentor melting into light and dissolving into you from the crown of your head, and visualize your body appearing in the clear, empty form of Vajrasattva. With undistracted, utterly free awareness, nakedly place your mind in the illusory-like nature of appearances without inhibiting their arising.

THE ACTUAL PRACTICE

Apprehending the Dreams

During the daytime, sustaining
mindfulness without distraction

Apart from the power of mental imprints, (phenomena) do not exist.

All avenues of appearances, negative and affirmative,

Are dream-like, though they are apprehended as external phenomena.

Without distraction, earnestly and continually sustain your mindfulness and attention (to this truth).

In solitude earnestly generate a sense of disillusionment with respect to death and impermanence and the suffering of the cycle of existence. Sincerely cultivate overwhelming compassion by thinking, "All phenomena are like illusions devoid of true existence, but these sentient beings do not know that and thus wander in the cycle of existence – beware!" As before, pray to your spiritual mentor with sincere reverence, asking, "May I apprehend my dreams and train in the illusory body of the dream state," and with a sense of fervent reverence, regard the present, seemingly substantial appearances as shrouded displays of appearances that are devoid of true existence. These good- and bad-appearing objects, as well as all mind states of apprehending them as negative and affirmative, are experienced due to the power of the deceptive manifestations of imprints placed upon the mind. Apart from that, there is not even an atom that truly exists.

Thinking, "These (things) that appear are appearances, but they are not truly existent," bear in mind that, in general, nothing is truly existent and, in particular, recognize (events) as dreams. Thus, establish single-pointed meditative equipoise in the awareness, "I have fallen asleep. This appearance is a dream. It is an illusion. I have certainly fallen asleep." Subsequently reflect, "There is death in all sorts of activity, in walking, lying down, sitting, eating, speaking and so on. Come what may, it is pointless." Never parting from the vision of your spiritual mentor, abide in sincere reverence. Especially, strongly project the thought, "I have fallen asleep. This movement, too, is a dream.

By continually practicing in that way, at all times during and after formal meditation, appearances will always seem devoid of true existence and of fear. Furthermore, place your awareness in a non-conceptual sphere, without focusing it anywhere. Then direct your mind to all the appearances of yourself and others and think, "All these are just appearances. They are not true." In particular, forcefully, without distraction, cultivate the sense that, "I have fallen asleep. All these appearances are just a dream."

At night strongly disciplining yourself in the quintessential instructions
Lie down to sleep with the resolve to apprehend your dreams.
Let your behavior be unhurried and calm, and as for the mind:
In your heart (imagine) a white, stainless AH (ཨ)
Sending forth varicolored rays of light,
Which melt samsara and nirvana into light and dissolve them into the AH.
Fall asleep with the sense of a clear vision,
Like the moon rising in a stainless sky.
It is sure your dreams will be many and they will be clear.

In the evening when you are about to sleep, meditate on the guru, and with sincere reverence pray, "Tonight may I dream many dreams – clear dreams, good dreams – and may I recognize the dreams as dreams," or "May I apprehend my dreams."

Prepare for sleep with unhurried behavior, in order not to disturb your channels and energies. In terms of the body, fall asleep in the cross-legged posture, in the posture of a sage, or in the "sleeping lion position," with your head supported and facing north, with the right side of your torso facing down. In terms of the object, in your heart appearing in the clear emptiness of your own body in divine form, clearly stabilize your mind in the visualization of a white syllable AH of the nature of stainless light. Abide with reverence for your spiritual mentor and the aspiration to recall your dreams. From the syllable AH are emitted rays of light of five colors like the light of a rainbow, and they pervade all appearances. Reflect, "They are all a dream." Imagine that those rays of light dissolve the appearances of all phenomena in samsara and nirvana into shimmers of light and think of them as a dream. Imagine that they are then drawn back and dissolve into the AH at the heart. Direct your attention to the syllable AH as to the radiant image of the moon rising in a clear sky. From that space, direct your mind to the clear syllable AH without grasping onto it. By falling asleep in that way, you will have many clear dreams, and you will apprehend them thinking, "This is a dream."

Here there are two sorts of experience. Apprehending a gentle dream entails thinking, "This is a dream" and many periods of deep sleep. Apprehending a rough dream involves nightmares such as falling off a cliff or being chased by a dog, and knowing, "This is a dream." If you do not apprehend them that evening, wake up and reflect, "At dusk I had such a dream, but I didn't apprehend it." Look ahead and meditate on phenomena as illusory. Thinking, "Now, by all means I shall apprehend the dream," meditate on the previous object and fall asleep.

If you still do not apprehend the dream, try the following. In terms of the time, there is the first light of dawn, dawn, and sunrise. Wake up at the end of the night, when you still need a little more sleep. Place your body in the proper posture and earnestly meditate on the previous object. When you arrive at any of the three periods, be in any of the three postures, and with the utmost clarity meditate on the previous object without grasping onto it. Fall asleep without letting any other thoughts intrude. In summary, by the power of continuous, undistracted mindfulness of the dream (nature of phenomena) throughout the day, both during and after meditation, when you fall asleep at night, the gross appearances of the waking state will vanish. Before you fall deeply asleep, there are the so-called thoughts between falling asleep and dreaming, sound faintly heard in the ears, the sense of the body becoming torpid, being pressed into darkness, and deep breathing. Right after there is a sensation of numbness at the point midway between the eyes, there will occur unclear, vague thoughts of people, the environment and so on. They are the cause of dreams, so if you recognize them, like inserting a thread through the eye of a needle, you will continue to dream. At that time, without opening your eyes, retract your "posterior energy," and direct your imaginative attention towards the dream without becoming diffused into the waking state.

For the superior person it is possible to practice like that. If upon engaging in the practice repeatedly like that, you do not apprehend the dreams, your mind has become diffused. Here there are four sorts: (1) empty diffusion as a result of not being inclined to dream, (2) disturbed diffusion when there are many dreams but you do not recognize them as such, (3) waking diffusion in the case that you wake up as soon as you apprehend the dream, and (4) lethargic diffusion when, immediately upon apprehending the dream, you get lost in an ordinary dream and slip into confusion. If you get into a habit in which any of those happen repeatedly, you need practical instruction on eliminating diffusion, and this you must know through oral guidance.

Training

Training in transforming the dream
When you apprehend (the dream) like that,
Reflect that all the appearances of the dream
Can be transformed in any way.
One can be increased to many,
Many can be reduced to one.
And peaceful and wrathful can be changed into
    each other.

Once you have become steady in apprehending your dreams, you should train in them. As an antidote to grasping at something as being one, you should train in increasing it. Meditate on the guru, praying that you may train in the dreams. Then by imagining that all appearances during the daytime are dreams, dispel all grasping onto them as being real. Think, "I have fallen asleep. All these appearances are the appearances of a dream. Since the appearances of a dream are not truly existent, they can be transformed in any way." When reflecting thus, practice moving gross and subtle appearances of sentient beings and the environment back and forth; increase one to many; gradually reduce many to one; transform pillars and pots and so on into living beings, both human and animal; within the environment and its inhabitants change living beings into pillars, pots and so forth just as you please; transform the peaceful into the wrathful and the wrathful into the peaceful and so on. Increase and transform in various ways whatever you like in whatever way you like. At night, recognize the dream as a dream, and with your previous imagination and objects, increase things as much as you wish, and change them in any way you like.

Training in the illusion
If upon dreaming of such things as fire, flood, and precipices, fear arises and obstructs your practice, calmly accept whatever comes your way, thinking, "I have fallen asleep. My actual body is on the bed. This body is a dream-body of mental impressions. These appearances, too, are appearances of a dream. Since dreams are not truly existent, being like an illusion, I can't be burned by fire or carried away by a flood." With a sense of carefree acceptance, enter into the raging fire and the raging flood, and strongly imagine the dream to be illusory.

Furthermore, reflect, "Dreams are deceptive appearances of the mind, and my mind is empty." Knowing this, abide in meditative equipoise on the inseparable union of the threatening appearances and your own mind.

Training in illusory liberation
In the pure and impure realms,
Dissolve beings and other phenomena and observe their mode of existence.
Attend like that, and apply it to the nighttime.
Whatever you see, bring forth your imagination.

The training in illusory liberation in order to cultivate noble qualities entails ascertaining objective appearances. One can observe the impure realms, including the abodes of gods and humans and so on, as well as all kinds of realms of hell, etc. One can receive spiritual teachings in the pure realm of Sukhavati from such buddhas as Amitabha, and one can meet one's spiritual mentors, wherever they are, and receive instruction from them as well. With the wish to observe the pure and impure realms and to see how individuals exist, meditate on the guru and pray to ascertain objective appearances.

During the day, direct your attention to the various realms you wish to observe and to whatever spiritual teachings you wish to hear; and at night know that you can apprehend your dreams and are able to do anything with them. By this practice, if you effortlessly and spontaneously see whatever you wish to observe and hear the spiritual teachings and prophetic indications that you desire, this is excellent. If this does not happen, during the daytime imagine either your own body or yourself visualized in another form as swiftly flying up into the sky, arriving wherever you wish, and seeing and hearing what you desire. By so doing, this will also happen at night in your dreams. At first this will occur only vaguely, but gradually it will become clearer so that finally you will know these things as they are.

THE ABSORPTION OF UNIFICATION

The absorption of unification with the pure illusory body
Then look upon your divine body as an illusion

And fall asleep strongly imagining this.
If, while sleeping, appearances of ferocious ani-
    mals,
Fire, flood, and other dangers arise,
With the sense that they are non-existent and
    merely appearances,
Meditate on them as being merged with your
    mind and on your divine body as an illusion.

Pray that your divine form in the dream may appear like an illusion. During the day, determine not only to apprehend your dreams, but repeatedly think, "To-night it's not enough to recognize my dreams as dreams. I must also transform the divine form of the meditation deity so that it is like an illusion, appearing but empty and free of clinging." If, while sleeping at night, due to some frightening apparitions you are effortlessly able to transform yourself into a divine form, this is best. If you are not able to do so, during the day think, "I have fallen asleep. These appearances are visions of a dream. Since dreams are deceptive appearances of my own mind, they can be changed in any way whatever. So now I shall transform them into the deity." Reflecting in that way, meditate on transforming yourself into a divine form. Thus, train in this illusory, dream-like imagination.

Meditate on the divine form appearing like a reflection in a mirror, without an inherent nature, clear and empty, free of clinging. By so doing, at night due to the appearance of frightening and amazing dreams, in your mind, your mind will naturally appear in divine form, clear and empty, without grasping, like an illusion. Then, by practicing transforming yourself into a variety of divine forms and increasing their number, all appearances will arise and increase in clear, empty divine forms.

> *The absorption of unification with the clear light*
> During the day, (think) 'This is a dream;
> It is emptiness, like space,'
> And place the illusion in the nature of clear light
> That itself is empty and clear, like space.
> From the sphere of lucidity you arise in divine
>   form,
> Increasing and transforming yourself and so on.
> Maintain this awareness during the day without
>   distraction,
> And at night apply the immutable essential oral
>   instructions.

Pray, "May I apprehend the clear light, and may I appear from the clear light in the divine form of union." During the day, while imagining the illusion of the dream, think with determined anticipation, "Tonight I shall place my sleep in the clear light, and from that I shall arise in divine form." Even if you appear in an ordinary way either in your own appearance or in divine appearance, by individually observing the appearance and the mind which produces the appearance, you will see them as illusions and grasping will thus be dispelled. In that very mental space immediately abide in meditative equipoise without the grasping of discrimination. Once the mind has dissolved into the clear light, pristine primordial awareness will spontaneously arise, like space – clear, empty and free from conceptualization.

Moreover, from that same mental space, practice arising in divine form, clear, empty and free of clinging, like a fish surfacing from the water. When you fall asleep at night, direct your mind to the tiny, radiant white AH at your heart, and place your awareness in lucid meditative equipoise, in clarity without grasping. Let your awareness become neither tense nor wavering. Meditating thus, when you fall asleep do not let thoughts intrude between the sleeping and dreaming states, and without wavering direct your mind to the AH. For ordinary people sleep takes place in the manner of obscuring the mind with darkness. But for those who have apprehended the clear light, like rays of sunlight cast upon a clear sky, all appearances arise in clarity, without conceptualization, joyfully and without clinging.

Furthermore, it is said that if you apprehend the clear light of light sleep, simultaneously with falling asleep you will have a sense of clarity and emptiness with just a little mental grasping; and if you apprehend the clear light of deep sleep, you will have a firm sense of abiding in non-grasping to clarity and emptiness like space. Thus, from the non-conceptual sphere of clear light you will arise in the divine form of union from the reverse sequence of appearances and energies. With this, train in strongly imagining increase, transformation, etc. during the day, as done before; and, at night, put the immutable pith instructions into practice. When you train in this way, divine forms will fill the space, without one obscuring the other; they will all appear without having an inherent nature; and they will be clear without conceptualization, blissful without clinging. They will appear with those three characteristics.

The absorption of unification with the intermediate state

If, during the night, you familiarize yourself with
the inseparability
Of the illusory body, the dream and the intermediate state,
Imagine the play of the spiritual body (dharmakaya) through the gradual dissolution
Into the ultimate clear light of death.
Imagine all self-arising deceptive appearances
As the arisings of the illusory fulfilled body (sambhogakaya).
Attend to the emptiness and lack of true existence of the entrance ways,
And thus train in the displays of the emanation
body (nirmanakaya).

Thinking in anticipation, "All appearances are like
illusions," or "At night in relation to the appearances
of dreams, I shall know the intermediate state as the
intermediate state," apprehend your dreams, and
think, "These are the appearances of the intermediate
state. I shall apply the practical instructions about the
intermediate state." By bringing to mind and meditating on the practical instructions about the intermediate stage, if you do not get lost in your dreams but
apprehend them, you will apprehend the intermediate state.

Now a person of finest sensibilities will be liberated
in this life and thus will not need to undergo the
bondage of the intermediate state.

Those of medium sensibilities will witness the signs of death and bring forth the spiritual body at the clear light of death. Then thinking in anticipation, "I shall arise in the illusory body of union in the intermediate state and shall serve the needs of sentient beings," they should repeatedly imagine, "This very appearance at the time of waking is the intermediate state." By bearing in mind that even in sleep and dreams there is the clear light and the intermediate state, and by meditating on the practical instructions, at the time of death they will dwell in the clear light of emptiness and bliss, their mind at death being the primordial awareness of the integration of the mother and child clear light. Then in place of the intermediate state, they will be liberated by the self-arising divine form of union.

There are three levels of people of inferior sensibilities. Superior individuals meditate on the inseparability of the illusory body, the dream and the intermediate state at all times, both while awake and while dreaming. If they become accustomed to this, finally at the time of death there will occur (1) the stages of dissolution of appearances of objects of the six fields of visual form, etc., (2) the stages of dissolution of the gross elements of earth into water, etc., and (3) the stages of dissolution of gross and coarse conceptualization. Following the dissolution of the "appearance," "expansion," and "attainment," the spiritual body of clear light will arise without creation. From the unimpeded play of the spiritual body, the fulfilled body will arise of itself spontaneously; and, due to this, the emanation body will mature and liberate sentient beings by means of the power of its enlightened activity.

Middling people, not having purified the three
appearances and not knowing the illusion-like nature
of reality, bring forth from the clear light the three
appearances together with the four elements in reverse order, and they take a body in the intermediate
stage that arises from the four subtle elements. From
this point they attend to the emergence of the appearances of the intermediate state and develop strong
disillusionment with them. Praying to be liberated in
the fulfilled body of the intermediate state, they individually inspect themselves and whatever else appears to them and reflect, "I have died. These appearances are appearances of the intermediate state, so I
shall train in recognizing the intermediate state for
what it is." By thinking in anticipation, "I shall place
this mental body of the intermediate state in the clear
light, and from that I shall arise as the fulfilled body,
the illusory divine body of union," they will arise in
the self-appearing fulfilled body.

Inferior people experience fear in the intermediate
state and craving for a place of rebirth. When, out of
craving and aversion, they consider, "I have died,"
they should not be afraid. Rather, they should think,
"Alas, since taking birth due to craving and aversion
is great misery, now I shall go to a pure realm!" and
they should pray to be liberated in the emanation
body in the intermediate state. It is best if they realize
the emptiness of the entrances to rebirth and thus
block them. The middling approach is for all the
appearances of the intermediate state to appear from
oneself, and by the power of seeing all self-appear-
ances as being like illusions, without true existence,

one stops them by transmuting appearances, sounds, and motion into deities, mantras, and emptiness, respectively. The inferior approach is to block evil rebirths by pure conduct, going for refuge, and so on. With powerful imagination, thinking, "I shall go to a pure realm!" they should depart the intermediate state with the practical instructions of "transference of consciousness" and the anticipation of prayer. Upon taking birth in Sukhavati and so on – realms of the natural emanation body – they will be liberated.

By practicing in that way one will accomplish the illusory body of union in this very life. Even if the illusory body is not accomplished, by repeatedly cultivating faith and devotion toward one's spiritual mentor, maintaining a sacred outlook toward the environment and its inhabitants and rousing the sense of the lack of true existence of phenomena, corresponding mental imprints will be stored. With such imprints, it is then possible to attain liberation in the intermediate state in one of three ways, according to one's sensibilities.

Be mindful in that way again and again,
And look upon the environment and its inhabit-
    ants as a palace and deities.
Finally you will arise as an illusory body,
But you will have personal freedom in the inter-
    mediate state.
Having heard and retained the oral transmission
    of the profound meaning
Of the practical instructions, from the platform of
    my senses,
I offer the turning of the wheel of dharma

To the glory of fortunate trainees.
By the merit of receiving this, may all animate
   beings
Purify the two obscurations and all mental im-
   prints,
And may they swiftly, without difficulty, attain
The primordial awareness of clear light and the
   illusory body.

*At the request of the elucidator of the teachings of the
earlier translations, the supreme emanation body Künzang
Padma Lekdub, I, the foolish monk (Lochen) Dharma Shri
received the above teachings from my spiritual mentor
(Terdag Lingpa) and presented them as notes. May they be
flawless!*

Translator's note: The author of these notes, Lochen
Dharma Shri, lived in the latter half of the seventeenth
century and received the above teachings from his brother
and spiritual mentor, gTer bdag gling pa, the founder of
Mindroling Monastery. In the spring of 1990, I received the
oral transmission and explanation of this text from the
Venerable Gyatrul Rinpoche. In October 1990, I completed
this translation with the invaluable corrections and suggestions of Gyatrul Rinpoche, Khenpo Gyurme Samdup
and Sangye Khandro.

                                        B. Alan Wallace

Part 2   The Commentary
       by Venerable Gyatrul Rinpoche

Oral Commentary to the Root Text on Releasing Oneself from Essential Delusion

The teaching here today on dream yoga concerns six different intermediate states that occur in cyclic existence, which are called bardos. If one has received these teachings and successfully prepared oneself through practice, then to accomplish this "bardo of the dream state" is to simultaneously prepare oneself for all "bardo states." The similarity of the bardo states cannot be underestimated when you take into consideration the repetitive cycles of conditioned existence. The dream bardo stands out as a separate state or experience with which you seem to be very familiar. In this teaching you should merge that familiarity with reality.

   This particular dream yoga teaching is based on a treasure of Vajrasattva that belongs to the well-known tertön Terdag Lingpa. It was written down in the form of notes by the great scholar Lochen Dharma Shri and is a well-known practice in the Nyingma tradition. The title of this text is *Releasing Oneself from Essential Delusion*. The release of oneself from delusion is an ongoing process as long as you remain in a state of impure awareness. These notes that comprise the root text for this practice instruct you in how to release the mind from impure awareness according to Vajrasattva's mind accomplishment of the dream state.

The text begins with the author's homage and then the statement of his commitment. The author pays homage to the guide and spiritual mentor Vajrasattva in the first stanza of the root text. This text provides a brief instruction on how to accomplish the mind of Vajrasattva by way of apprehending and transforming dreams. The teaching is divided into two parts: the preparatory part of the training and the actual training itself.

The preparatory stages of the training involve the preliminary practices, called ngöndro. The ngöndro is likened to the preparation of a field for planting crops. Initially, you prepare the field as best as you can, removing all the unwanted weeds, stones, boulders and so forth, making the soil as fertile, rich and workable as possible. This is the same procedure needed in spiritual training. In order to prepare the field of your mind according to this system, you perform the preliminary practices. The preliminary practices employ specific skillful methods to weed out the grosser delusions in the mindstream and prepare the mind for the stages of practice and realization that follow, such as deity generation, dissolution, the Great Perfection, and so forth.

Many of you are very unstable in your practice and in your life in general, with many highs and lows, like a teeter-totter. The main reason this occurs is because you lack the foundation necessary upon which to build stability. You have failed to cultivate a pure, clean field, the mindstream, that you can then apply to the practices. This is best done by accomplishing the preliminaries. Many people, even after ten years of practice, will find that they are still not making that much progress and that they still have an abundance of obstacles and doubt. The only reason for this is their failure to prepare the field of the mind, which is in fact the accomplishment of the preliminaries prior to moving on to higher, more advanced techniques which the mind is simply not ready to receive.

This is true not only for Buddhist practitioners, but also for Christians, Muslims, Hindus and all practitioners of the great religions of the world. The basic principles and precepts of all true religions are very pure. What you see as impure is simply the inability of those who adhere to them. So as Buddhists, for instance, if you fail to embrace and internalize the basic principles and precepts of the practice, then your mind is always going to be overrun by the five mental afflictions. These negative afflictions are desire, hatred, jealousy, pride, and ignorance. They are the basic obstacles which impede you from making any true progress on the path. It is, in fact, the function of the preliminary training to prepare the field of the mind so that you are actually able to put to rest the gross delusions and give rise to your innermost qualities. This allows you to actualize your true bodhicitta nature, the mind which cares about others more than self.

Leaving aside the idea of the so-called spiritual path, or religion, if you are able to uproot these delusions, the stones and boulders, from the field of your mind, then you will become an honorable person, respected in the world, with an easier, flexible attitude toward yourself and others. If you are able, through your development of wisdom and skillful means, to unite the teachings with your life, then true results will be achieved. This begins with knowing the cause for non-virtue or the accumulation of negative karma. With an understanding of what the ten non-virtues are and that they arise as the result of the presence of the five mental afflictions, you come closer to an accurate understanding of the source of your delusion. Taking rebirth in any of the six states of rebirth is the result of these causes. Depending on the motivating force and degree of intensity of the cause, rebirth is taken either in the hell, hungry spirit, animal, human, jealous god, or long-life god realm.

Now you might be thinking, "What is he talking about?! We don't know that these so-called realms really exist (except for maybe the human, animal and perhaps the spirit realm)." Indeed these realms are just as real as your present experience of this one. They are places where countless beings experience various inconceivable numbers of life forms. Leave aside the others and look at your own realm – the human realm. The most fortunate rebirth of all of these six classes is certainly that of a human being, but among human rebirths, the best is that of a precious human rebirth. It is considered to be extremely fortunate to possess a precious human rebirth with the eight freedoms and ten endowments.

Of the eight freedoms, four are external and four are personal. You need to examine to see if you possess them because, if you do, it means that you are in a state of total freedom to practice on the spiritual path with the full potential to achieve liberation in this very life. The first external freedom (the freedoms from rebirth in other states) is, specifically, freedom from rebirth in the hell realms. All states of rebirth are created by the mind and arise as the projection of mental habituation, and the hell realms are no exception. In this experience beings must endure unbearable heat and intense cold, with no interlude, for the duration of time that their karma confines them.

The second is freedom from rebirth in the hungry spirit realm where beings suffer from constant, insatiable desire. Such beings are never free from the sensation of tremendous hunger and thirst. The third freedom is from rebirth as an animal. Since you can see the animal kingdom, you know the lack of freedom and karmic restrictions the animals bear – for instance mistreatment by humans, preying on one another, living in a state of fear and anxiety and stupidity to the point where it is virtually impossible to be liberated from cyclic existence as an animal. The fourth is freedom from rebirth as a god, be it titan or deva. Generally, in the state of existence of the gods, there is no opportunity to consider spiritual practice or liberation simply because of the overpowering influence of pleasure and other states of preoccupation. If you are not experiencing rebirth in any of these four states, it means you possess the four external freedoms.

The four personal freedoms are, first, freedom from birth in a barbaric land, for instance a Communist country where one is only able to hear incorrect, mistaken views and never has a chance to be introduced to any religious belief. The second is freedom from rebirth as a person holding incorrect views so that one is unable to appreciate or trust in the truth when it is heard – for instance, maintaining the view of an atheist with no interest or ability to hold religious views. The third freedom is from rebirth in a place where even the sound of religion is never heard because it simply does not exist there. The fourth is freedom from being born with mental incapacities or retardation in which one is simply not able to comprehend the meaning of truth and put it into practice. Now, if you possess the eight freedoms, you are extremely fortunate.

What causes the eight states of non-freedom? The basic state of delusion, lacking awareness of one's own innate awareness, or wavering from that, entering into a state of delusion and accumulating negative karma based on that delusion, produces all of these various unwanted results.

The ten endowments also pertain to you both circumstantially and personally. They include birth in a land where there is exposure to the dharma or religious traditions, birth with all mental faculties intact, birth with a mind that possesses irreversible faith in the infallible law of cause and result, birth during a time that the Buddha's teachings exist in the world, birth in a situation whereby one meets with a true compassionate guide who leads one upon the path, and so forth. When you consider whether you possess these eighteen qualifications of a precious human rebirth or not, it becomes clear that probably all of you here do. Now you must recognize that this is definitely the result of a tremendous accumulation of merit and practice over countless past lifetimes as well as in this very lifetime. These are results that you are presently experiencing which are extremely fortunate. What would it be like if you didn't possess this? What would it be like if you were experiencing a different situation? You have to consider that, if you lack these freedoms and endowments, it means you possess an abundance of negative karmic accumulations instead. At least at this time, you can consider that you have an abundance of positive karma and merit of which you are experiencing the immediate results. You need to appreciate it and embrace it as the single most important possession in your lives. Other things in life you cherish are not nearly so important, like good looks, money, position, and charisma. In actuality, and particularly according to the spiritual path, these things are of no importance whatsoever.

In one way worldly qualities are important temporarily, but consider where all those good-looking and rich people go when they die. Eventually they must pass from this life. I don't really need to tell you the answer. Think carefully for yourself, "What happens to all the pretty, important, and rich people?" Obviously their lives are impermanent, as all lives are. What you need to consider is that your present situation of freedom and endowments is not going to last forever. In fact, you have no idea when it will be over. You should consider that all animate beings, as well as all inanimate things, are subject to the truth of impermanence. Look around your world at the other cultures and countries and the different calamities that are constantly occurring. Clearly you can see impermanence in constant action.

Especially you must look at yourself. When standing in front of the mirror, take a good look. If you look at others, you can see impermanence; but, until you apply it to yourself, it won't really matter. It must hit you that you are losing yourself, your own personal situation which, according to the path, is a very rare and precious state of freedom and endowment. With each and every day, a part of this chance slips away.

If you wish to travel to a land far away and need a suitable vehicle to transport you there, yet you just ignore the vehicle and still wish very much to get there, it's kind of futile, isn't it? In the same way, if you wish to achieve liberation and the only suitable vehicle that will bring about that result is the precious human body, to ignore the opportunity at hand and postpone the seizing of this opportunity is a great mistake.

Do you know someone who can help you to get there? According to Buddhism, that someone is Lord Buddha Shakyamuni. The reason is because the Buddha is one who first brought himself there; he actually went through the stages on the path and became enlightened, thus becoming known as the Buddha, the Fully Awakened One. As an awakened being who has achieved that state through his own efforts, he has all of the capabilities to show you the path unmistakably through his precious teachings, the Dharma, that comprise the path to liberation. Those who uphold the teachings and follow the path are the Sangha, the other buddhas and bodhisattvas, or the spiritual community comprised of practitioners on all levels of awareness from bodhisattvahood and arhatship on down. These are the Three Jewels of Refuge: the Buddha, Dharma and Sangha.

If I were to elaborate on the subject of the preliminary practices, it would take me an entire week. It's too bad there's no time because I like to talk about this; however, we have only one short day to cover the main topic, the apprehension of dreams. I'll begin with that now, but please do consider the importance of these preliminary contemplations to this and all practices.

As you begin your practice of dream yoga each day, reflect on your own death. Recognize that, wherever you are born in cyclic existence, be it high or low, its very nature is saturated with discontent and suffering. Seeing that cyclic existence is pointless, you should restrain your mind with a powerful sense of disillusionment; and, in that sense of powerful disillusionment, you should allow the mind to remain in pure awareness. In this state of pure awareness, begin to see your dwelling place as a pure realm which is an expression of your mind's nature.

Imagining your dwelling place to be a pure realm, visualize in the space in front of you, on a high and broad throne, the appearance of your own spiritual teacher in the aspect of Vajrasattva. Consider that Vajrasattva is the condensed essence of all objects of refuge and the nature of Vajrasattva is that of your own spiritual guide. Then, think to yourself, "I and all other sentient beings, fearing the misery of cyclic existence, seek refuge, and it is only the object of refuge who knows the true nature and can guide and liberate me." Recognize as well that all parent sentient beings have, at one time or another in your countless past lifetimes, been kind to you just like your own present-life mother and father who have given you your life, have given you food and drink, and have expressed nothing but kindness towards you. In order to repay that kindness, you should arouse from your hearts a sense of overwhelming compassion and love for all beings and make a vow to personally liberate them from their suffering and bring them to the attainment of perfect awakening. Make the commitment that, for this reason, you will practice the profound path of dream yoga.

This age-old analogy of the kindness and love that a father or mother has for his or her child sometimes hits the American mind and heart a little bit incorrectly. This is because a lot of people feel that they were abused by their parents or as adults they don't have a good relationship with their parents. So when they hear "all parent sentient beings" and then "at one time or another every living being has been your mother or father and you should repay their kindness," they think of their own mother and father toward whom they harbor hatred, anger and frustration. This is very incorrect because, no matter what has happened through your childhood or even your adult years, it is in fact your parents who gave you the body that you now possess; they gave you your precious life. You should, at least, consider how kind they were to nourish you when you were very young and care for you until you were able to survive on your own. Without your parents of this life, you wouldn't be here. When you feel that type of aggression toward your own parents, you need to consider, "Do I love my own children or not?" If you have children, how do you feel about them? How do you care for them? The love that parents have for children and children for parents is unconditional and extremely sacred. You should not defile it with ordinary mental afflictions.

In most cultures in the world, particularly in the Tibetan culture, this is definitely not a problem, and the parent-child relationship is honored as the prime example for developing immeasurable love toward others. If it is still a problem for you in this culture, then think about your loved ones, those whom you do love – perhaps it's your boyfriend, girlfriend, wife, husband – think about those beings and how kind they have been to you and what joy they have brought you. Then imagine all living beings to be just like that.

Now as you focus with pure awareness upon Vajrasattva in the space in front or above the crown of your head, give rise to a state of fervent devotion to the point where your hair stands on end or tears spontaneously fall from your eyes. Then begin to earnestly pray that you may have many clear, lucid dreams and that you may be able to apprehend your dreams and gain the potential to transform dreams into beneficial experiences for the sake of benefiting others. By making strong prayers in this way, finally you should consider that Vajrasattva, as your root teacher, melts into light and dissolves down into you and that you then become the clear, empty form of Vajrasattva. In that state of awareness, simply remain in undistracted, fresh, pure perception with an apprehension of the illusory nature of all appearances. This completes the preliminary stages to the actual dream yoga practice.

The second part of this practice, the actual dream yoga, is practiced according to your own stage of development. Each stage naturally leads to the next experience. The first stage is the teaching on apprehending dreams. After you become adept at dream apprehension, you enter upon the second stage, which is to train in transforming dreams. This then leads to the remaining stages of development, the training in the absorption of unification. Each of these three stages has sub-stages of corresponding development.

Concerning the first stage – the apprehension of dreams – there are two parts beginning with daytime practice. During the daytime, one must sustain mindfulness without distraction. This mindfulness is to constantly remind oneself that all daytime appearances are nothing other than a dream. Throughout the different experiences during the daytime reality, you just keep on mindfully sustaining the awareness, "This is a dream, this is a dream, I'm asleep and I'm dreaming," and this will create a habit. The second stage is that, at night, you must strongly discipline yourself in the quintessential instructions. The mind must be strong enough to take the quintessential instructions, which is what you are receiving now, and apply the instructions in the midst of a dream. For instance, even if you are having a nightmare or some frightening experience, the mind must be able to apprehend that it is a dream although the experience seems to be intensely real.

This daytime training is called "sustaining mindfulness without distraction during the daytime experience." It should be clear that this does not mean you are sleeping. This practice occurs when you are awake and going about the usual routine of a day. You must simply remind yourself again and again that you have fallen asleep and that your experience is a dream, in order to establish the habit of lucid dreaming.

Then you are ready to begin the practice for nighttime, which is the application of strong discipline in the quintessential instructions. Even though you may be feeling quite sleepy or uneasy, you should not be too anxious to fall asleep immediately. Take a few moments to calm and center the mind. The root text says, "Lie down to sleep with the resolve to apprehend your dreams. Let your behavior be unhurried and calm. As for the mind, in your heart imagine a white, stainless AH (ཨ) sending forth varicolored rays of light which melt samsara and nirvana into light and dissolve them into the AH. Fall asleep with the sense of a clear vision, like the moon rising in a stainless sky. It is sure your dreams will be many and they will be clear."

After calming the mind, meditate upon the guru and recall the kindness of the lama as mentioned before. In a state of sincere devotion and reverence, you should continue to pray in the following way: "Tonight may I dream many dreams. May I have many dreams, and may my dreams be very clear. May they be very good. May I recognize the dream as a dream. Simply put, may I apprehend my dream." With that prayer in mind, as your final thought, you should try to fall asleep either in the sitting meditation posture, the sage or rishi posture, or the posture known as the "sleeping snow lion."

The meditation posture is called the seven-point posture of Buddha Vairocana and requires legs crossed right over left in the full or half lotus position, a straight spine, relaxed arms, hands right over left in your lap, chin tucked in slightly, eyes gazing out over the tip of your nose and the tip of the tongue touching the roof of your mouth. This posture is to be maintained until you naturally fall asleep; and if thereafter the posture shifts, it is no longer relevant. The rishi posture is to sit with knees up parallel to the chest, right leg crossed in front of left with crossed arms (right over left) and elbows touching knees with fingertips touching opposite shoulders. Feet are flat on the ground. The third, most popular option is the sleeping snow lion posture. Here you are on your right side with right hand under your head (or pillow), knees tucked in slightly with left arm extended down the side of the body. This is the posture assumed by Lord Buddha Shakyamuni when he passed into parinirvana.

It is most important not to be hurried so that you do not disturb the natural, subtle flow of the body's energies. It is ideal if your head points to the north with your face toward the west. In terms of the body, this is how you should position yourself to fall asleep. In terms of the mind, you should consider that, in the center of the physical location of your heart, a clear, empty syllable AH appears which is clear white and luminous. Do not forget to maintain pure awareness of self-nature as the embodiment of primordial wisdom (the deity). You should allow your mind to remain in equipoise upon this stainless white syllable AH.

At this point, once again you may invoke the blessings of the lama by recalling his or her kindness. Inspired by pure faith and devotion, once again state your aspiration to recall and apprehend your dreams. With that as your final thought, from the syllable AH, five-colored rainbow light rays radiate to encompass all of phenomenal existence. Imagine that there is no place where the rays do not pervade. All appearances become like five-colored rainbow light. Consider that all appearances are just like a dream and that all the light rays and patterns are but a dream. Then consider that all the light rays dissolve all appearances of samsara and nirvana into shimmers of light which are also like a dream. Imagine then all appearances as shimmering light being drawn back to reabsorb and dissolve into the AH in your heart. Then focus solely upon the syllable AH appearing lucidly like a radiant image of the moon rising in a clear sky. At this point the mind is concentrating solely upon AH, without grasping, simply remaining aware. By falling asleep in this way, you will have many clear dreams, and you will apprehend your dreams, thinking, "This is a dream," while you are in the middle of it, or just shortly after it begins.

As soon as you apprehend your dream, two sorts of experiences may occur. The first experience is apprehending what's called a gentle dream. This entails thinking, "This is a dream," and then having many periods of deep sleep which follow the thought, "This is a dream." Apprehending a rough dream, which is the second experience, involves nightmares such as falling off a cliff or being chased by a wild animal or a ferocious dog and, while in the middle of that experience, still apprehending it as a dream. This is what is called apprehending a rough or coarse dream.

If you do not apprehend the dream, when you awaken, reflect, "At dusk (or whenever it was) I had such a dream, but I didn't apprehend it correctly." Then you should look ahead and meditate on all phenomena as illusory in the same way that you had been doing before, and you should re-establish your commitment. Think, "Now, by all means, I shall apprehend the dream without any distraction." Then just as before, by employing the methods, fall asleep and try again.

If it occurs that you still do not apprehend the dream, then you should try the following. In terms of time, there are three periods to consider: the first light of dawn, dawn, and sunrise. During any of these three times, when you are still able to sleep longer if you awaken, then you should position your body and earnestly meditate upon the AH in your heart and perform the same procedure again. Generate a very strong resolve that you will indeed apprehend your dream.

In short, if you are unable to apprehend your dreams in a normal sense after numerous attempts, then try to make use of any one or all of these three periods of time. Do not forget the three physical postures as well. The meditation remains the same in all cases. The most important thing to bear in mind is to maintain awareness of AH without any mental grasping and to fall asleep in that state without letting any other thoughts intrude. You must try to fall asleep before the intrusion of mental distraction. By continuous, undistracted effort and mindfulness of the dreamlike nature of daytime phenomena, both during and after meditation, when you fall asleep at night the gross appearances of the waking state will vanish. This is the key point: to maintain the daytime awareness to a point where gross appearances will vanish so that you can apply the method and fall asleep without the intrusion of ordinary, coarse discursive thoughts.

Before you fall into a deep sleep, there are so-called thoughts between falling asleep and dreaming. Before you actually fall asleep and you are still in the process of falling asleep, thoughts arise and sounds are still faintly heard. You have a sense of the body's becoming very torpid and a sense of becoming pressed into darkness. You also have a sense of the experience of deep breathing as you begin to relax. Right after that, there is a sensation of numbness at the point midway between the eyes. At that time, you will begin to feel vague impressions of people, animals, environments, or whatever your recent mental impressions are. These vague mental impressions are the cause for the dream. The dream you will have actually arises as the result of these impressions. If you recognize this, it is your chance to recognize the dream, like threading a needle right through the eye, and you will immediately enter the dream and apprehend it.

This is called a bardo or intermediate period, because, when the dream phenomena begin to arise, your state of awareness moves from the waking state to the dream state. The last indications before this are the vague impression, the numbness sensation, the torpid feeling, and so forth that were just explained. In particular, it is the vague mental impressions which then uncontrollably become the dream state, like a thread going into the eye of a needle. This is almost identical to the stages of dissolution that occur when the intermediate state of your current birth changes to the moment of death. The moment of death is identical to falling asleep in that sounds are faintly heard, the body becomes torpid, and mental impressions are vague and unclear. Although you may be surrounded by people as you approach the moment of death, the mind is no longer able to grasp onto the fading objective appearances of that life. Then you enter into the moment of death.

If you are able to come to a dream by moving the mind from the vague mental impressions into the dream state by recognizing that that is the cause of the dream, you will be able to apprehend the dream. It's important at that point that you don't open your eyes or become distracted by the diffusion of awakening. If you do awaken, then the experience stops and you are prevented from moving on into the experience of the intermediate state of dreaming. It's also useful to bring up your posterior wind by closing off the lower orifices and drawing the energy up in the body, keeping your eyes closed and experiencing the dream without diffusion.

A person with superior capabilities will be able to practice accordingly and experience results. Otherwise, if you find that you are still unable to apprehend your dreams, it means that you are suffering from diffusion. According to this practice, there are four different states of diffusion. The first is empty diffusion, an experience in which you are not inclined to dream and so you simply do not dream.

Therefore, there is nothing to apprehend. This presents a problem since you are thereby unable to train in this practice Usually this indicates that the mind is so diffused or scattered that it is not contained in a point at which a dream can occur. The second is disturbed diffusion, an experience in which you have many dreams but are not able to recognize them as such because your mind is too disturbed. The third is waking diffusion in which you wake up as soon as you apprehend the dream. In the moment right after you apprehend the dream, you awaken, which prevents you from training any further. The fourth is lethargic diffusion upon apprehending a dream – the mind then gets lost in the dream and skips into confusion. Here the mind is so lethargic, sluggish, or deluded that, although you apprehend the dream, it just continues on and you slip into ordinary phenomena in the dream state, which shifts into confusion, thereby preventing you from carrying out the training.

If you get into a habit in which any of these four diffusions begin to occur and re-occur, then it means that you need to receive practical instructions on how to eliminate this habituation to diffusion. That kind of practical instruction can only be received through an oral transmission given by a qualified teacher. It is extremely important to seek out such guidance when it is necessary.

The second stage is the actual training which follows the apprehension of dreaming. Once you've been successful in apprehending your dreams, then you must train. The training occurs in three parts which are also stages of development. The first stage is the conscious transformation of dreams. This includes dream creativity and transformation. Here you can change the dream into whatever you wish. The second stage is the training in illusion, and the third is training in illusory liberation.

In the section on training in transforming the dream, the root text states, "When you apprehend a dream like that, reflect that all the appearances of the dream can be transformed in any way. One can be increased to many, many can be reduced to one. Peaceful and wrathful can be changed into each other." Once you are apprehending dreams with confidence, training is performed to clear the mind of negative habitual patterns in much the same way that you practice to purify negative tendencies during the waking state. For instance, an antidote to the mind's tendency to grasp onto an experience as being real is to intentionally increase it into many. This dissolves the need to grasp onto that particular appearance.

In this way you train to improve your own awareness while in a lucid dream. Here you should continue to pray to the guru and practice guru yoga, shifting the emphasis of the prayer to accomplish the stage of training that you've reached. By praying to the guru to be able to train in the dreams, imagining that all appearances in the daytime are dreams and telling yourself that you are asleep and in a dream, you will complement your practice with mindfulness while awake.

At this time, since you have apprehended that the appearances of the dream have no true inherent existence, you begin to reflect on the practice of moving things back and forth, shifting and changing them, transforming them at will. The gross and subtle aspects of the imagination or of phenomena are easily transformed in the dream state, and you can even exchange sentient beings for inanimate objects. Basically, whatever you want to do, you'll have the ability to do because it's all lacking true or inherent existence anyway. In other words, since it is a dream, it can be changed and it will be changed. You must proceed with confidence and try it out. One dream can be increased to many; many can be reduced to one. You can exchange pillars for pots and pots for pillars; you can exchange animals for humans and humans for animals. Just proceed to transform all those illusory appearances any way you like. You can transform peaceful into wrathful, wrathful into peaceful, and so on and so forth. This practice also encourages the flexible, supple nature of the mind to manifest. With your previous imagination and objective impressions, you may proceed to create whatever wholesome experience you would like to have. This is basically what this stage of training is all about.

This training in transforming the dream leads to the second stage of training in the illusion. For training in illusion, you should consider that if you dream that you are being carried away in a flood, burning in a fire, falling into a ravine, or experiencing some other type of danger, then you need to calmly accept it as it is occurring and enter into it as being illusory in nature. At the time that you are actually endangered, rather than trying to stop or change it, accept it by entering into it. That is best accomplished by thinking, "I have fallen asleep. My actual body is on the bed. This is just a dream experience. This body is a dream body of mental impressions. Appearances, too, are dream appearances. Since dreams don't have any true, inherent existence, there is no possibility for the fire to really burn me or hurt me; there's no possibility that I will drown or be carried away by this flood, or that my bones are going to be broken when I fall down this ravine, because this is just a dream." Strongly ascertain the illusory nature of dreams. Training in the illusory awareness of phenomena in general is very useful, but specifically here you must train during the apprehension of a dream. Due to this awareness of illusion, fear dissipates and there is no need to avoid anything. Otherwise, those would have been frightening experiences. In addition to that, you should reflect that dreams are deceptive appearances of the mind and that the mind's nature is that of emptiness. Since the dream is just the arising of deceptive appearances, allow it to dissolve back into its empty source, which is the nature of the mind. In this way, there is nothing threatening about the appearances other than the fact that it's simply your own mind. Your own mind should not be a threat to you.

The third stage is training in illusory liberation. As the root text states, "In the pure and impure realms, dissolve beings and other phenomena and observe their mode of existence. Attend like that and apply it to the nighttime. Whatever you see, bring forth your imagination."

This practice, which is slightly different, is done by examining objective appearances in order to develop noble qualities and specifically to cultivate a state of liberation that occurs through illusory awareness. In this context, you can observe impure realms, like the realms of beings in the six classes: gods, humans and the like, as well as pure realms such as the realms of the buddhas and bodhisattvas, Amitabha's pure realm (Dewachen) and so forth. Your spiritual teachers who have passed away can all be experienced again by accomplishing the experience of training in illusory liberation. You can meet with spiritual mentors and spiritual friends and receive additional training in the dream state. Now in order to accomplish this, once again you need to meditate on guru yoga and make very strong prayers to be able to see how individuals exist in pure and impure realms. Through your meditation upon guru yoga and the force of prayer, these appearances will become apparent.

During the daytime, you should focus on whatever hidden passions or desires you may have in order to observe various realms of existence. For instance, while practicing, allow the mind to enter more natural states of awareness and then make prayers to observe various realms or to receive different types of instructions from different spiritual mentors. At night you should know that, if you're able to apprehend your dreams, then you can do anything with them. If you have a wish in the daytime that you want to enter into the pure realms and receive teachings in those realms, then you need to bring that wish directly into the dream state, apprehend it and create it. Basically, that's how it's done.

Individuals with superior awareness will effort-lessly and spontaneously accomplish this because of their previous habits and the rapid ripening of their prayers. If this does not occur and you find that you are having difficulty, then during the daytime you need to imagine that your own body is a pure illusory form (such as that of your own meditational deity), that you are flying swiftly up and throughout space, going here and there with very supple flexibility. If you imagine that you have these powers very strongly during the daytime, then at night in your dreams – because dreams are just extensions of daytime habitual tendencies – the same phenomena will occur. At first this will occur only vaguely, but gradually it will become more and more clear until the experience seems as real as you think ordinary daytime experiences are.

Here there is a pitfall to be avoided, namely the tendency to develop spiritual pride. For instance, if one has been able to apprehend a dream, transform it into a visitation with a buddha or a journey to a pure realm, then one may also develop a strong tendency to want to boast about this accomplishment to others. There are many who are inclined to very quickly express what they think is a spiritual accomplishment to others, saying, "Oh, I was able to fly into space in my dream, and I had this accomplishment," and so on. The problem with that is, inasmuch as it was able to occur due to an ungrasping mind, if you then allow the grasping mind to cling to that state, you have created a stronger habit of grasping than you had before you started, which will completely block any further spiritual development. It is like building a big wall on the path. If you boast about your accomplishments in the dream state to people who have accomplished identitylessness of self and who keep their spiritual insights private, then they are easily able to see your impeded state of awareness. Inasmuch as you are probably trying to impress such people (whether they are your mentor or not), you will surely make a fool of yourself, unbeknownst to yourself. It is much more useful to remain silent.

Until now we have covered the first two general stages in dream yoga development: dream apprehension and training (on various levels). The third section is the absorption of unification. In the absorption of unification, there are three additional stages of development: unification with the pure illusory body, unification with clear light, and unification with the intermediate state (bardo).

We begin with the absorption of unification with the pure illusory body, as the root text states, "Then look upon your divine body as an illusion and fall asleep strongly imagining this. If, while sleeping, appearances of ferocious animals, fire, flood, and other dangers arise, with the sense that they are nonexistent and merely appearances, meditate upon them as being merged with your mind and meditate on your divine body as an illusion." Here, as before, you need to pray that your divine form in the dream may appear like an illusion, and you need to meditate upon your body as a divine form as you are going to sleep, making the prayer that it may appear as an illusion. During the day, you must not only determine to apprehend dreams, but to think repeatedly, "Tonight it's not enough to recognize my dreams as dreams; I must also transform the divine form of the meditational deity so that it is like an illusion, appearing empty and free of clinging."

If, while you are sleeping at night, you are able to take a frightening apparition, something terrifying, and effortlessly transform it into a divine form (that of the deity), then this is suitable for accomplishing this stage of the practice. In fact, this is the best.

To be able to effortlessly transform a frightening apparition into the divine form of the deity is excellent. If you find that you're not able to do that, then the other way to approach it is to remind yourself again during the day, "I've fallen asleep, I'm dreaming. These appearances are visions of a dream. Since dreams are deceptive appearances of my own mind, they can be changed in any way whatsoever (which is similar to what we've already covered); so now I shall transform these appearances into the form of the deity." Reflecting in this way, you meditate upon transforming yourself into the divine form of the deity and train in the illusory, dreamlike imagination. You can meditate upon the divine form appearing like a reflection in a mirror in order to understand the illusory nature. Think of it as being like a reflection in a mirror, or like the reflection of the moon in a clear, still body of water. Imagine that it has no true, inherent existence; it is simply luminously clear and empty. Think that this is the very nature of appearance. By creating this habit again and again in the daytime through imaginative techniques, at nighttime you will have a stronger habit and a stronger ability not to be frightened during nightmares. Rather, at the moment of that apparition, simply see it as the illusory form of the deity with which you have previously been working.

This particular stage of the dream yoga training corresponds directly to the bardo of intrinsic reality which occurs after the bardo of the moment of death.

After the subtle mind has separated from the body, the mind (which is a mental body now) experiences itself beginning to travel through the intermediate state, separated from a gross corporeal body. However, it still carries with it the same mental impressions. Therefore, if through training in the dream state, you have the ability to recognize yourself as the illusory form of the deity, you can then multiply the appearance of that form into countless impressions of peaceful, expansive, powerful, or wrathful embodiments – whatever you wish to create. Likewise, in the bardo, all of these types of phenomenal projections will arise from one's own mind. They will be recognized as manifestations of illusory form, and all fear will dissolve in that moment. Herein lies the key to liberation in the bardo of intrinsic reality – recognizing that all is merely a projection of one's own mind.

The second stage to this unification is unification with clear light. This is simply a deepening of the awareness of the nature of the mind. As the root text states, "During the day, think, 'This is a dream. It is emptiness, like space.' And place the illusion in the nature of clear light that itself is empty and clear like space. From the sphere of lucidity, you arise in divine form, increasing and transforming yourself and so forth. Maintain this awareness during the day without distraction, and at night apply the immutable, essential oral instructions." In order to unify with the clear light in the dream state, again you should maintain special prayers related to this particular accomplishment: "May I apprehend the clear light, and may I appear from the clear light in the divine form of union."

As you can see, the training of dream yoga corresponds to the other stages of the bardo because all are interrelated, almost identical experiences. In fact, you are dealing with the same mind. The mind just continues on through different intermediate periods. You have already moved through experiences which are likened to the bardo at the moment of death and the bardo of intrinsic reality, and this point of unification with clear light closely resembles the bardo of seeking rebirth in which the mind is about to be brought back into an embodied form. In order to consciously experience that in the dream state, from clear light the divine form needs to re-emerge. Clear light arises from the empty nature. The nature of emptiness is luminosity. The union of emptiness and luminosity is expression, and it is from that seed of expression that the divine form is born. In regard to this, you must have determined anticipation and the strong prayer, "Tonight I shall place my sleep in clear light awareness, and from that clear light I shall re-emerge as the divine form of the deity."

Whether you appear in your own appearance or in divine appearance, by individually observing the nature of the appearance and the mind producing the appearance, they will be seen as an illusion and grasping will be dispelled. If you watch both the appearance and the mind that is apprehending the appearance, whether the appearance is pure or impure, and if you apprehend that both are illusory, grasping and clinging will automatically be dispelled. In that very space void of grasping or clinging to subjective self or objective phenomena, by abiding in meditative absorption upon the nature of the mind, the clear light unification will spontaneously manifest. This experience self-originates. When the mind is finally free from conceptualization and discrimination, the nature of mind is exactly like space. The spaciousness of that nature is empty; it has no boundaries or limitations and is luminously clear and utterly open. This is how you will experience the nature of your mind.

When you are abiding in the nature of mind, the manner in which the illusory form arises from the mind is similar to the way a fish suddenly emerges from water. The spontaneity of your appearance as the illusory deity will arise from the clear, empty nature of the mind as simply and suddenly as a fish emerges from water. Direct your mind into the tiny, radiant AH which is right in the empty center of your heart (core of your being); and placing your awareness in clarity without grasping, without tension or wavering, abide gently with awareness until you fall asleep. If you're able to fall asleep in that state, this corresponds to the place in between thoughts.

In between each thought formation, moment by moment, there is an empty state where the mind is in its natural state. This corresponds to the moment after you fall asleep and before the dream appearances arise. Having just fallen asleep, once the waking appearances subside and before the dream appearances begin, the experience is empty, clear, and open. Similarly at death, when the elements have dissolved and the subtle mind separates from the body, there is an experience of space before entering into the bardo of intrinsic reality. This is the very moment that the appearances of the past lifetime cease. Before the bardo appearances begin, there is empty, open space.

This is the space that you need to actualize and maintain. Each morning when you awaken, this space is again experienced. When dream appearances end and before you awaken, that moment in between is the empty clear nature. Recognize it. Again, in between thoughts, when one discursive thought ceases and before a new one arises, the clear, empty nature is manifest.

The crucial point here is to fall asleep without any mental fixation or grasping, remaining aware of the syllable AH in your heart and not allowing other thoughts to intrude in between the point of falling asleep and dreaming. By maintaining awareness of AH, the thoughts are prevented from intruding as one naturally enters that empty, clear, open space. Ordinary, untrained, deluded people will fall asleep in the manner of obscuring the mind with darkness. Due to the mind being obscured with darkness, the dreams become meaningless floods of past events and habitual concepts and so forth, which produce nothing more than additional conceptual attitudes. This is ongoing. Otherwise a deep sleep may occur like a deluded state of darkness. For a person with training, who has been able to ascertain the clear light, or the nature of mind, even a little bit, the experience is more like the sun shining in a clear sky – everything is luminously lit up and very, very clear, experienced without any grasping and with total joy. This is the experience of a person who falls asleep successfully through this method.

There is a subtle difference that may occur here based on apprehending the clear light in a light sleep or a deep sleep. If when you fall asleep your sleep is light and you've fallen asleep with an awareness of AH and with all of the teachings intact, you enter into your experience of clear light; but, because your sleep is very light, there is still a subtle grasping that occurs. If you fall into a deeper sleep with the clear light awareness, there will be no grasping or conceptualization at all, and it will be the experience of deep meditative equipoise on the nature of emptiness which is the nature of clear light.

From this non-conceptual sphere of clear light, you will experience yourself spontaneously arising as the divine form of the deity. Just as awareness of self nature as the deity dissolved into the open, empty expanse of clear light, you now re-emerge as the expression of pure divine form. By ascertaining emptiness and clarity, the illusory divine form is naturally manifest. From that, countless manifestations of oneself as well as other appearances arise as the display of clear light without any stain or mental obscuration. This experience is endowed with the qualities of emptiness, clarity and bliss.

The third unification is the unification with the intermediate state or bardo. This bardo is understood as analogous to the experience before your next lifetime. As the root text states, "If during the night you familiarize yourself with the inseparability of the illusory body, the dream, and the intermediate state, imagine the play of the dharmakaya through the gradual dissolution into the ultimate clear light of death. Imagine all self-arising deceptive appearances as visions of the illusory sambhogakaya. Attend to the emptiness and lack of true existence of the entrance ways, and thus train in the displays of the nirmanakaya."

Here, to begin the training, you are preparing for the intermediate state, which is the state after your death. You should think with anticipation that all appearances are like illusions, which is similar to what you've been doing all along. Or you may think at night, in relation to the appearance of the dream, "I shall know the intermediate state as the intermediate state." Apprehend your dreams and think, "These are the appearances of the intermediate state." Within apprehending the dream, imagine that these dreams are none other than the intermediate state, the bardo. Furthermore, have a strong conviction that you will apply the instructions that you have received from your spiritual mentor about the intermediate state at that time, bringing to mind the practical instructions about the intermediate state during the dream state.

If you do not get lost in your dreams and are able to apprehend them, then you will also apprehend the intermediate state. It stands to reason that you will do so. Rather than a dream, you are apprehending what is an experience of the intermediate state to you. For people with sharp faculties, there is no need to train in any of this, because they will actually be liberated in this life through the force of their daytime and nighttime practice. They will not need to consider the intermediate period because liberation will occur prior to this time. People of middling faculties will be able to witness the fact that they're dying, to directly confront it, and enter the stages of dissolution into the clear light experience. That clear light experience will be in accordance with their practice and from it they will arise in the illusory body of union in the intermediate state.

However, people who are able to give rise to the illusory body of union in the intermediate state must also bear in mind that, even in sleep and in dreams, they're experiencing the clear light in the intermediate state. By meditating on the practical teachings that they've received from their spiritual teachers, at the time of their death they will dwell in the clear light as a blissful, empty experience. At death their minds will experience the integration of the mother clear light and the child clear light. These two clear lights will be joined again, like a child jumping back into the lap of its mother, and as they integrate to become a single experience, liberation occurs.

Now, regarding people of inferior sensibilities who are temporarily unable to accomplish liberation in the manner mentioned, there are three categories given. The superior-inferior will meditate on the inseparability of the illusory body of the dream and of the intermediate state. Through their sustained mindfulness most of the time in waking and dreaming reality, they will become so familiar with their practice that at the time of death, they will have the following experience: A normal dissolution will occur at the time of death, wherein the objective appearances of the six conscious states, such as visual forms and so forth, will dissolve into the organs, and the elements of the body will dissolve back into the basic elements of the universe – earth, water, fire, air and space.

During these stages of dissolution and finally as coarse conceptualization comes to an end, appearances will dissolve simultaneously as the white seed descends to the heart. Then the dissolution of expansion occurs as the red seed ascends to the heart. Finally, the dissolution called "near attainment" occurs when the red and white seeds mix together and the mind enters into a state of unconsciousness. A trained person (the superior-inferior) would then enter into the clear light. In the clear light one would realize the nature of the dharmakaya and that all appearances arise as sambhogakaya. Then from the sambhogakaya, by the force of one's prayers and vow to liberate all sentient beings, the nirmanakaya will arise. Here the arising of the nirmanakaya is the intentional direction of the consciousness to assume an embodiment for the sole benefit of others. This is the manifestation of the power of concerned activity.

The mediocre-inferior would be those people who have not yet purified the three visions to be understood as illusory nature, dream, and the intermediate period. Having failed to purify these three, they will not know the illusory nature of reality encompassed by illusion, dreams, and the intermediate state. Without this training, they cannot realize that all appearances are an illusion. Therefore, when they pass from this life, they are unable to be liberated in the clear light at the moment of death. They then go on into the bardo of intrinsic reality, where again phenomenal projections begin to arise. It is there that they begin to recall their training from the immediate past life and a very strong sense of disillusionment with these appearances arises. Although they are unable to ascertain the true nature of the appearances, the degree of disillusionment that is experienced prevents them from experiencing attraction or attachment. Then they pray to be liberated in the bardo of intrinsic reality;

and, by the force of the prayers and teachings they have received in the past as well as their own awareness of what appears to them, they reflect, "Now I've died, I am dead. I am in the intermediate period. I am no longer with my body; my body is dead and has been left behind. I'm a mental body traveling in the bardo. I need to pray to be liberated at this time. I need to pray to recognize the nature of all these appearances to be the nature of the sambhogakaya deity." In this state of prayer, by giving rise to pure awareness, when the mind merges with the nature of the appearance, liberation occurs.

The most inferior person will be one who experiences fear in the intermediate period at the time of the arising of appearances and apparitions and fails to go into union with the sambhogakaya presence. Such a person will have a strong craving to find a place of rebirth. This craving arises due to the basic deluded habit of attachment to desire and copulation. The mind attaches to the intensity of that attraction. If the mind is more attracted to the father, then one will be reborn as a girl. If the mind is more attracted to the mother, then rebirth will occur as a boy.

Inferior people at this point in the bardo do have virtuous, positive mental impressions because they were practitioners from their previous lives. It may seem to them, at that point of intense habituation to desire that, "Oh! I have died! I'm dead; I'm in the bardo." If, rather than feeling fear, they are then able to consider that, "Yes, I'm dead. I'm a mental body in the bardo. If I take birth due to strong desire and sexual attraction, this is a cause for great misery. This is the very reason that I have been conceived into rebirth after rebirth. This is the play of samsara, and now I must reverse this. This is my last chance." At this point, if prayers are made to be reborn in a pure realm and to be in the presence of Buddha Amitabha or any buddha for whom they have the strongest affinity, liberation in the nirmanakaya (embodiment of intentional manifestation) will occur before actually being conceived into another rebirth in cyclic existence.

In this moment there are three possibilities which again correspond to the degree of one's mental training and development. At this very point, individuals with superior sensibilities would be those who have in some way or another ascertained the view of emptiness. Because they have that view of the nature of emptiness, then they enter into the view and are able to obstruct the door to future rebirth. When ordinary appearances cease, this is one way to stop the cycle of rebirth taken in an ordinary sense. Persons of intermediate sensibilities recognize at that moment that all appearances are their own projection and have no true, inherent existence. They ascertain all appearances as the play of illusion and enter into the awareness of all form as the deity, all sound as mantra, and all thought as the arising of the mind of primordial wisdom. These are the three vajra states. In that awareness, the door to ordinary rebirth is closed. Inferior persons recall their pure conduct and refuge from the past life.

For instance, if one has been ordained, one may recall those good habits which also have the power to obstruct negative tendencies. Based on that, one may be able to then think, "I shall go to a pure realm rather than taking an ordinary rebirth." If one has been fortunate enough to receive and accomplish the practical instructions on the transference of consciousness (given by one's spiritual mentor during the past life), then this technique, known as *phowa,* can be performed. At that very moment in the bardo, one will transfer awareness to a pure realm.

From that pure realm, such as Sukhavati, Amitabha's paradise, or whichever, one will then be liberated. Once arriving in a pure realm, one does not fall back into cyclic existence, and liberation is gradually realized. Even the inferior person is able to achieve liberation in this way. Through training one will be able to accomplish the absorption of unification in these different ways. If accomplishment of this level does not occur, it is still very important to bear in mind the importance of cultivating faith and devotion toward the spiritual mentor as well as an aspiration to cultivate pure vision by transforming the environment and its contents into a pure realm and the illusory expression of the deity. This is done by constantly reminding oneself that there is no true, inherent existence to any aspect of subjective or objective appearances. Such potent mental imprints will at one time or another bring you to the state of liberation. Then it is entirely possible that liberation will occur during the intermediate state in any of these ways mentioned.

In conclusion the root text includes a prayer which reads,

Be mindful in that way again and again and look upon the environment and its inhabitants as a palace and deities. Finally you will arise as an illusory body, but you will have personal freedom in the intermediate state. Having heard and retained the oral transmission of the profound meaning of the practical instructions from the platform of my senses, I offer the turning wheel of dharma to the glory of fortunate trainees. By the merit of receiving this, may all animate beings purify the two obscurations and all mental imprints, and may they swiftly, without difficulty, attain the primordial awareness of clear light and the illusory body.

PART III
MEDITATION

The Illumination of Primordial Wisdom
An Instruction Manual on the Utterly
Pure Stage of Perfection of the Powerful and
Ferocious Dorje Drolö, Subduer of Demons
by
His Holiness Dudjom Rinpoche,
Jigdrel Yeshe Dorje

Translated by
B. Alan Wallace

Commentary by
Venerable Gyatrul Rinpoche

Translated by
Sangye Khandro

Part 1 *The Root Text*
by His Holiness Dudjom Rinpoche,
Jigdrel Yeshe Dorje

The Illumination of Primordial Wisdom
An Instruction Manual on the Utterly
Pure Stage of Perfection of the Powerful
and Ferocious Dorje Drolö, Subduer of
Demons

Namo Maha Guru Vajrakrodha Lokottaraye!

There are two parts to this instruction manual on the utterly pure, profound stage of perfection, which is an essential treatise on the powerful accomplishment of the very secret, powerful, and ferocious Dorje Drolö, subduer of demons: the preparation of establishing the basis of quiescence; and the main practice of cultivating the primordial wisdom of insight.

THE PREPARATION OF ESTABLISHING THE BASIS OF QUIESCENCE

From the primary text:

> The profound stage of perfection involves
> Directing the spear of your combined energy and
> awareness
> Exclusively at the red HUM[1] at your heart.

In a solitary place free of human distractions and without disturbing noise and so on, firmly compose yourself on a comfortable cushion in the erect, straight, cross-legged posture having the seven qualities of Vairocana. With respect to speech, let your breath be normal. With respect to your mind, without letting your mind indulge in any activity of dwelling on the past or pondering the future, etc., cut off conceptual elaborations concerning the three times, and place your attention in a non-creative, undistracted state.

If you can abide in that state, that is fine. If you cannot, imagine at your heart the syllable HUM filled with the color red, of any size that you find appropriate. Let this image arise vividly, without forcefully grasping it with your mind, and with complete attention focus on this clear image by naturally letting your awareness settle upon it.

If you also find it difficult to rest your attention on this, place in front of you a small or large object, such as a drawn syllable, a stick, or a pebble. Then direct your visual gaze upon it, without moving your eyes or eyebrows. Do not bring to mind any discrimination of good or bad mind states and so on, and without imagining anything, cast off all concerns and settle your awareness in this state.

From within that mental state, whatever conceptual appearances arise, do not follow after them; but, applying yourself to the meditative object, focus your entire attention upon it without conceptualization and without distraction.

If your attention becomes dull, lift your gaze, firm up your posture, and stimulate your attention. Bring forth an energetic awareness, and gaze at the object single-pointedly.

If your attention becomes scattered and agitated, lower your gaze, relax your posture, relax deeply, and let your awareness rest in a natural state.

Similarly, apart from your awareness of distinct sounds, pungent smells, and your natural respiration, do not reflect on anything, but place your attention upon the object in a relaxed way. Or, it is also suitable to place your attention immediately without any object, or upon some other object.

By meditating in this way, at the beginning you may think there are many appearances of conceptualizations, but without looking upon these as either virtues or vices, continue to meditate, and by so doing they will gradually become pacified. Then joy will arise in your body and mind, your mind will be unable to rise from the stability of this non-conceptual state, and you will abide single-pointedly and continously, without any desire to move. These are the signs of familiarization with quiescence.

THE MAIN PRACTICE OF CULTIVATING THE PRIMORDIAL WISDOM OF INSIGHT

Coming to a Conviction by Means of the View

Establishing the nature of objects, which are apprehended as external

Demons, hindrances, and spiteful and malevolent spirits –
All these are nothing more than appearances of the mind.

All animate and inanimate phenomena, including oneself and others, and things that are designated and characterized as obstacles, demons and hindrances, seem to be truly existent. However, apart from the deceptive appearances of one's own mind, there is nothing whatever that exists in reality. Things do indeed appear, but they are not real. Regard these as illusory hallucinations, like the appearances of a dream which do not, in fact, exist, and see them simply as random, unconnected appearances.

Moreover, apart from mere designations, their nature is beyond the conceptual elaborations of existent and non-existent objects. Thus, do not view them in reality even in the manner of apprehending them as illusions. In this way come to the conviction that all these appearances are illusion-like primordial wisdom, which is self-appearing and without distinction.

Establishing the nature of the mind, which is the internal apprehender

Recognize the mind free of characteristics.

In terms of the body, establish the seven qualities of the proper posture. In terms of the speech, let your respiration proceed naturally. In terms of the mind, let it be neither tense nor slack. Without bringing anything to mind, place your awareness in an uncontrived, relaxed state. With your attention directed inward, focus completely on the mind's own nature. By so doing, there will arise a "self-clarity" that is without object, free of the extremes of conceptual elaborations, and free of any sense of apprehender and apprehended, including any viewer and viewed, experiencer and experienced, and subject and object. Freshly enter into meditative equipoise in that very state, without contriving anything, contaminating, or changing it.

The above is the meditation technique for those of superior faculties, and it brings one into the general nature of essential awareness. Most people will find it difficult to encounter essential awareness in this way, for their minds are disturbed by compulsive ideation. So, by following after essential awareness alone, seek out the mind.

Furthermore, if now and again you become distracted by deceptive thoughts, follow them and observe whence they first arose, where they now exist, and where they finally cease. Moreover, what are these agents of joy and sorrow, including those who wander in the cycle of existence, all the way up to those who are becoming spiritually awakened? If you think that agent is the mind, ask yourself, "Does that mind have a beginning, an end, and an intermediate phase? Is the mind itself a thing or not a thing? If it is a thing, what kind of a shape, color, etc. does it have?"

If you think that it is not a thing, repeatedly ask yourself, "Does it not exist at all, or what is the case?" Examine these issues without forsaking the task at hand.

If you think there is such a thing as this, you have fallen to the reification of grasping onto true existence. If you think it does not exist at all, that it is empty, you are simply speculating. If, as a result of not finding the mind, you conclude that it is utterly non-existent, or if you feel that it must exist but you cannot decide whether you have identified it or not, continue investigating and questioning.

If you do not perceive either the observed or the observer, the seen or the seer, and so on; if by means of your investigation and examination you find nothing, in much the same manner as you see nothing by looking into space; and if primordial awareness appears nakedly and serenely, divorced from any recognition of the nature of the duality of appearances and cognition, unmediated, inexpressible, inconceivable, unobservable, empty and clear, without an object – in this event you have internalized the instructions.

Ascertaining the view of the nature of reality
Emptiness and clarity are the ultimate Drowo Lö.[2]
Do not seek it elsewhere but in this unmediated, Self-arisen, primordial awareness –
The great omnipresent Lord of Samsara and Nirvana.
Return to this great, primordial place of rest.

In this way, one is freed of all characteristics of elaborations concerning the apprehender and apprehended objects. One recognizes the primordial nature of awareness, empty of any intrinsic identity, the place of rest that is pure from the beginning and beyond thought and expression. One recognizes the self-display of primordial wisdom, which is clear, radiant, and unimpedable, as the spontaneously existent, great, omnipresent Lord of Samsara and Nirvana. Moreover, the nature of reality is the non-composite place of rest, primordially free of the duality of apprehender and apprehended. Awakened from the beginning, unmediated, this self-arisen, primordial wisdom abides in itself. The recognition of knowledge of the exhaustion of all phenomena is the view of the Great Perfection, which transcends the intellect. Realize this through an authentic encounter with it.

Practicing by Means of Meditation

The past has ceased, and the future
Has not arisen. Bring the consciousness of the present,
As unmediated, empty awareness, onto the path.

Recognize for yourself that the dharmakaya is none other than this great, empty, clear, self-arisen awareness which transcends the intellect. Do not create or alter anything in the momentary consciousness of the present in which past thoughts have ceased and later ones have not arisen. By so doing, settle your ordinary consciousness in its natural, uncontrived state, uncontaminated by conceptualizations concerning the three times, altogether free of the dimension of time. Come to the firm conviction that the technique of meditation entails nothing whatever apart from this.

Come to the innermost liberation of the realization that everything that appears is the welling up of the dharmakaya, and the realization of empty awareness that is unmediated and free of the intellect. Upon this basis, casually settle your consciousness in a state of effortless relaxation, like space, free of extremes.

At that time, while the objects of the six senses do appear, let your awareness be self-illuminating, utterly unmediated, and free of grasping. Inwardly let your mind be devoid of conceptual, discursive elaborations and withdrawals, and be self-awakened without mediation. Even when awareness abides in its own state, it is not bound by antidotes; but left as it is, it remains uninfluenced by good and bad objects. Do not contaminate it with grasping. Without letting the intellect intrude with its antidotes for countering obstacles, recognize the unadulterated facet of awareness. Cultivating your awareness in this way, without obstruction or mediation, is a quality of the Great Perfection.

Sustaining Continuity with One's Behavior

In this way if you find stability through
   familiarity. . .

During meditative equipoise, casually release your self-illuminating, empty awareness, without contaminating it with grasping or clinging to unmediated, primordial wisdom. During the period after meditation, without grasping, decisively ascertain all appearances as being clear and empty like illusory apparitions or the appearances of a dream. By applying this to the spiritual path, meditation and post-meditation sessions become indivisibly integrated. Since all appearances manifest as personal liberation, conceptualizations will arise as aids to meditation. If you are afflicted by conceptualizations, direct your full attention to whatever thoughts arise. By so doing, thoughts will vanish without a trace, like waves disappearing into the water. Once the conviction arises that conceptualizations are without any foundation or essence, the cultivation of your practice will proceed joyfully. In short, during all your activities do not let your ordinary mind succumb to the onslaught of delusion, but practice the yoga of unwavering non-grasping continuously, like a river. In this way you will come to the culmination of familiarity with the practice.

The Manner in Which Fruition Is Achieved

Once all phenomena with characteristics have
    been overwhelmed,
The glorious heruka will become manifest.

Spontaneously present awakening is one's own pure awareness, which has never been deluded. But by immediately clinging onto the characteristics of deluded thoughts, which do not exist as they appear, awareness is obscured, and one is captivated by the view of searching for awakening elsewhere. Due to the kindness of one's spiritual mentor, one is introduced to the nature of the dharmakaya, which dwells within, and one rests in the cultivation of the realization of primordial liberation. Thus, without fabricat-

ing any new attainment, the primordial nature mani-
fests as it is, and this is called the fruition of the
practice. Having become empowered in the attainment of the wrathful heruka, the omnipresent Lord of
Samsara and Nirvana, one will spontaneously engage in effortless, boundless, enlightened activity.

Colophon

*Due to the encouragement of Tsewang Paljor, the teacher
from Nyö, and many other aspirants to this path, I, Jigdrel
Yeshe Dorje, have composed these concise, clear instructions so that they can be easily understood firsthand. May
there be victory!*

Translator's note: In July 1990, I received the oral transmission and explanation of this text from the Ven. Gyatrul
Rinpoche. In October 1990, I completed this translation
with the invaluable corrections and suggestions of Gyatrul
Rinpoche, Khenpo Gyurme Samdup, and Sangye Khandro.

B. Alan Wallace

Part 2   *The Commentary*
by Venerable Gyatrul Rinpoche

Oral Commentary to the Root Text on the Illumination of Primordial Wisdom

The subject that we are going to discuss concerns a combination of topics which are quite unique. The topics are the union of mahamudra and mahasandhi as applied to the practice known as shamatha meditation or quiescence. These pith instructions have been condensed into a manual which was written by H.H. Dudjom Rinpoche, one of the greatest Buddhist scholars of all time. Because of his tremendous scholarship, he had the unique ability to be able to condense this type of material into short, comprehensive practice instructions which are as straightforward as they are deep. It seems appropriate to offer this teaching to you at this time, and please do understand that this is something very precious and rare.

Although this subject is the essence of the pinnacle instructions on the Buddhist path, it is important to understand that this must be preceded with a foundation. You cannot expect to be able to actualize that which is so profound if there is no basis or ground. There must be an entranceway before you can enter a building; before you reach the highest step, you must step upon the steps that precede it.

One of the main points of contemplation in establishing the foundation is the consideration of your condition as sentient beings existing in the round of birth and death. This state of cyclic existence that you are in as human beings is but one of the six classes of existence. Although you are unable to perceive the higher god realms and the two lowest realms, you can see the animal realm as an integral part of your own human realm. Clearly you can see how animals must endure suffering due to their many limitations and mistreatment imposed by human beings. Human beings on the whole must endure the four great rivers of birth, illness, aging, and death. Perhaps it is difficult to really believe in the other realms of existence. As Buddhists you must trust in the words of the Enlightened One, Lord Buddha himself, who, upon his own awakening, delivered his first discourse on the subject of the four noble truths based on his own experience and omniscient wisdom. In having seen the condition of cyclic existence that is by nature that of suffering, wherever you're born in any of these six classes, inevitably you will experience suffering rather than happiness.

The different states of rebirth and circumstances that beings in the six classes experience are totally dependent upon karmic accumulations, the infallible law of cause and effect. The actions of the past produce the result of the future place of rebirth and the circumstances associated with the birthplace. Generally speaking, the cause for rebirth in the two god realms is the accumulation of negative karma motivated by pride, arrogance, jealousy, or aggression. The circumstance of the rebirth is thereby that of constant warfare, competitiveness and, in the case of the long-life gods, a very blissful and happy life until the karma is exhausted. Seven days before the gods pass from that realm, they perceive their future place of rebirth in the lower realms. At this point they are powerless to reverse their karma because their time as a god is exhausted and new merit was not accumulated. As everything around them begins to wither and die, they suffer tremendously because they have used up all of their good karma and have no storehouse for that type of rebirth again. As human beings, you suffer at the time of birth, when you are ill, as you grow old, and of course at the time of your death. Animals suffer from stupidity and mistreatment and the necessities of survival. Hungry spirits suffer from intense thirst and hunger, hell beings from intense heat and cold.

Among beings in these six classes of rebirth, those in the human realm experience the least amount of suffering. However, human beings, in order to really be able to practice the dharma, must be born with freedoms and endowments. Just possessing a human rebirth in an ordinary sense is not enough; you must have a precious human rebirth. You must have freedoms and endowments, such as having your sensibilities intact and birth in a country where you can hear the dharma, where you can actually practice, where you can meet with compassionate spiritual teachers, and so forth. It is essential that you have these freedoms; otherwise the opportunity for achieving liberation from cyclic existence will not arise.

With these freedoms and endowments, you are then in a position to achieve freedom or ultimate, permanent happiness in this very body, in this very lifetime. On the other hand, if you misuse such an opportunity, through this very body you can accumulate karma which produces the result of lower rebirth.

How is it, then, that you should proceed on the path to total, ultimate freedom? It should be done according to the example that Buddha Shakyamuni has given you. By recognizing your precious opportunity, this precious human rebirth so difficult to obtain, you then follow the path as the first priority in your lives and achieve the result that you wish to accomplish. In this way you become like the great bodhisattvas or accomplished masters, male and female alike, whom you admire. In fact, they are no different from you. The opportunity that you have right now is the same opportunity that they had. The difference is that they actualized the full potential of their opportunity until the ultimate goal was realized. You should not see yourselves as being different from the greatest masters or bodhisattvas of the past. There's really no difference at all. They were human beings with a precious human rebirth, just like you are. Contemplating the suffering of cyclic existence and the precious human rebirth which is so difficult to obtain inspires you to seize this rare and precious opportunity, yet it is the contemplation of impermanence that truly motivates you to begin practice immediately.

Since you cannot guarantee how long your life will be, you have no idea how long this precious human rebirth will be yours. Because wherever you are born in cyclic existence is the result of your karmic accumulations, you begin to realize that, even though you have this potential, you must make use of it immediately. You also begin to realize that it is extremely difficult to consider getting out of samsara without someone to guide you. Until now you have been unable to liberate yourselves without a guide. It's very important that you find a spiritual teacher who is qualified and willing to help you achieve freedom.

According to Buddhism the best spiritual guide is the Buddha as the teacher, the Dharma as the path, and the Sangha as the best spiritual companions to befriend you upon the path. All schools of Buddhism take refuge in the Three Jewels as the external sources of refuge. As you go deeper on the path, the refuge becomes more internal. According to the hinayana and mahayana schools, refuge is always taken in Buddha, Dharma and Sangha. As you enter vajrayana or secret mantra, while refuge is taken in the Buddha, Dharma and Sangha according to one's level of understanding and practice, refuge is also taken in the Lama (the spiritual teacher), the Yidam (meditational deity) and the Dakini (the female principle of enlightened awareness).

As the understanding of this inner refuge deepens (according to maha yoga practice), refuge is then taken in one's channels, vital energies and essential fluids (according to the mother tantra anu yoga). As this process deepens or becomes more internal (according to ati yoga or the vehicle of the Great Perfection), refuge is taken directly in the mind in its essence, which is empty; in its nature, which is radiantly luminous; and in its quality, which is unobstructedly compassionate.

Why are these different aspects of taking refuge necessary? Because this is a natural development that occurs. As the view of one's own nature as a buddha develops, one's innermost qualities arise spontaneously, like a child who is growing up. When you enter the spiritual path, at first your focus is more external. This is natural because as beginners you need to relate to it in that way. Gradually, as you begin to deepen, the focus becomes more internal and less emphasis is placed on the objects existing outside of yourselves. Initially, the objects are your guides and then slowly, slowly you come to see that in fact it is your own true nature that is your guide. At first you wish to emulate your guides, but eventually you recognize that in fact this is your own nature. Step by step your focus moves from outer to inner as you come to understand that the Three Jewels are the channels, energies and fluids, and similarly the channels, energies and fluids are the manifestation of the essence, nature and qualities of the mind.

Oftentimes, the Buddhist religion is looked upon as a path of idol worship because of its strong external expression of devotion to the objects of refuge. Such devotion is necessary as long as dualistic awareness exists. Because of your habituation to grasping and clinging, it is necessary to worship or venerate the refuge objects outside of yourselves. Particularly in the lower schools of Buddhism, it is essential. For instance, as a fetus during the nine months in the womb, you are totally dependent upon your mother, and after you are born you are still dependent upon your mother. As you grow up and begin to mature, you become dependent upon your teachers, and eventually you become dependent upon yourself. What you are doing is developing those qualities within yourself. You cannot expect your mother or your teacher to take care of everything for you for the rest of your life.

On the spiritual path – that of inner pursuit – although it may seem that initially there is an external focus, eventually you have to recognize that all qualities must arise and be developed from within. Due to the kindness of your parents and the kindness of your teachers, you are able to come to recognize your own potential. When it comes to the task of liberation or enlightenment, you must recognize that enlightenment is already your own nature. It is the true essence of your own nature, like the sun. Similarly, the experience of cyclic existence occurs due to your own confused perception and mental afflictions. The mind that will achieve enlightenment is the same mind that has created this state of confusion. All images of the buddhas, all thangkas of meditational deities, all mandalas, statues, and so forth are used as supports through which the true nature of the mind may be actualized.

For instance, if you want to grow a flower garden or even one flower, you must have water, proper soil, and fertilizer. However, it is not the water and the fertilizer that produce the flower; it is the seed, the essence, which has the potential to become a flower. Just like that, your own mind – the nature of your mind – has the potential to either create samsara, as it has done, or to establish liberation, total freedom from all pain and suffering. However, it needs support. Just as a flower needs water and fertilizer, the mind needs the support of a spiritual teacher and practices on the path in order to get in touch with and actualize its true nature.

Once an understanding of liberation has been established, there are two ways to approach it. You can approach it according to the hinayana path, whereby you wish to achieve freedom for yourself alone, or according to the mahayana path, whereby you wish to achieve freedom for the sake of liberating all other beings. The latter is definitely the better approach, because it includes all living beings. Up until now, your focus has been wanting to accomplish only your own ends, always doing things with the motivation of self-interest. Because of that, you are still in samsara, still suffering, still full of discontent. This arises due to concern for oneself alone. The buddhas and bodhisattvas have dropped the concept of self and exchanged self-concern with concern for others; they always focus on the needs of others. They always consider, "What can I do to help others? What can I do to serve them?" With that as the motivating force, liberation from the bondage of suffering is easily achieved. This is a very important point to consider. As long as you grasp onto and cherish yourselves, you will remain in samsara; but, if you can reverse that focus and cherish and work for the welfare of others, this is the way freedom is achieved.

Developing the wish to liberate or enlighten all living beings is the initial stage of developing bodhicitta, the awakening mind. With that wish, you need to develop immeasurable impartiality, love, compassion, and empathetic joy for all beings and their deeds. Once these four immeasurables have been developed, you are ready to practice bodhicitta by engaging in the six perfections.

This has been a brief overview of the meaning and importance of the preliminary contemplations, as well as the basic taking of refuge and generation of bodhicitta. These practices are essential prerequisites to the practice of quiescence which is the main subject of discussion.

What is the benefit of peacefully abiding, allowing the mind to remain still, in a natural state which is motionless? Until you are able to develop quiescence, you will not be able to control or suppress deluded mental afflictions. They will continue to arise and control the mind. The only way to get a handle on that and put an end to it is to accomplish quiescence. Once that is accomplished, all other spiritual qualities will arise from that basis, such as superknowledge, clairvoyance, the ability to see into the minds of others, to recall the past, and so forth. These are mundane qualities that arise on the path but are developed only after the mind can abide peacefully. Qualities such as heightened awareness and clairvoyance must be developed, because it is through them that one is able to understand and realize the fundamental nature of the mind. As it says in the *Bodhicharyavatara*, one of the most important mahayana texts, "Having developed enthusiasm in this way, I should place my mind in concentration; for one whose mind is distracted dwells between the fangs of mental afflictions."

An individual who has been able to accomplish quiescence will no longer be overpowered by attachment to ordinary activities and contact with worldly people. The mind automatically turns from attachment and attraction to cyclic existence, because quiescence is the experience of mental contentment and bliss which is far more sublime than ordinary attractions that arise from confused perception. When the mind is at peace, it can then be directed to concentrate undistractedly for indefinite periods of time. Quiescence destroys delusion because mental afflictions do not arise when one is experiencing the equipoise of single-pointed concentration.

People who have achieved quiescence naturally experience compassion as they view the predicament in which other living beings are ensnared. Pure compassion arises as they begin to clearly perceive the nature of emptiness in all aspects of reality. These are only a few of many qualities as taught by the Buddha which are the direct result of accomplishing quiescence.

Quiescence is the preparation and basis for the main practice which is the cultivation of the primordial wisdom of insight. These two meditations are complimentary. The success that one has in developing insight is dependent on the success that one has with developing quiescence. If you are able to develop quiescence only to a certain degree, then your experience of insight will be limited. However, if you are able to fully accomplish quiescence, then you will be able to fully perfect insight as well. If that is the case, then that is as good as saying perfect enlightenment will be realized.

Now as for accomplishing quiescence, initially you should try to practice in a place which is isolated, quiet, and comfortable. It is important to feel comfortable and content in the place you have chosen to meditate. After arranging a comfortable cushion to be seated upon, assume a very straight sitting posture. The seven-point posture of Buddha Vairocana is ideal. Otherwise, be sure to sit so that the spine is erect. If you are sitting in a cross-legged position, then the best position to sit in is the full lotus. If you are unable to sit in full lotus, you can sit in a cross-legged position and elevate your buttocks a bit so that your back will be straight. Otherwise you may sit in a chair so that your back is straight. Keeping your spine straight, you should bend your head down a bit so that the chin is slightly tucked in and allow the gaze to go out over the tip of the nose. Allow the tip of the tongue to barely touch the roof of the mouth in a natural way so that the mouth is neither tightly closed nor gaping open. The arms and hands should be down to the sides. If you are sitting in a cross-legged position, the hands can be placed right over left in your lap. Otherwise, if you are sitting in a chair, they can hang naturally.

The sitting posture is very important and so is the position of the speech. Allow the speech to be silent – no talking, no making of sounds, just natural breathing. There is nothing else to do other than remain calm and natural.

The position of the mind is to avoid recalling events of the past, anticipating future events, and contriving or controlling the present moment. Just allow yourself to remain natural and at ease. Whatever arises should be allowed to be as it is without alteration or adjustment.

To "allow your mind to rest in the natural state" is easier said than done. The main reason for that is because, from countless past lifetimes until now, you have established habitual instincts, mental impressions that make your mind chaotic and full of countless varieties of conceptual proliferations. In order to achieve peace, you must employ techniques. This does not mean that you should try to control thoughts by recalling, anticipating, or altering the experience. But rather, as you begin, you should attempt to place the mind upon an object so that the mind can focus and calm down. The use of objects on which to place the mind corresponds to the three kayas. The first step is the nirmanakaya method and is accomplished by using an image of Buddha Shakyamuni appearing as the nirmanakaya buddha (embodiment of intentional manifestation). An image of Buddha Shakyamuni is positioned directly in front of you so that you will gaze naturally upon it.

The second step is the sambhogakaya method accomplished by using an image of Vajrasattva appearing as the sambhogakaya buddha (embodiment of complete rapture). The third step, the dharmakaya method, is accomplished by visualizing an image of Vajradhara in the center of the heart. Once quiescence is accomplished in these three stages, you are ready to begin quiescence practice with no elaborations at all.

If you do not possess any of these images of the Buddha, the practice can still be carried out. You may use a stone, a stick, a flower, or something natural that is found in the environment and that costs nothing. Simply practice with that object directly in front of you exactly as you would practice with the image. Ideally the object should be about four finger-widths wide. The mind should remain single-pointedly focused upon that object without any other distraction. While allowing your gaze to remain single-pointedly focused upon the statue or object, notice what your mind is doing while you are trying to focus. There should be no attempt to generate a visualization as you would in generation-stage practice. You are simply looking at the image with single-pointed concentration, nothing else.

When you are practicing for more extended periods of time, you may experience the mind becoming dull and sleepy. When that starts to happen – and it is a common reaction – you should straighten up your body, readjust your position, and move your gaze to the uppermost part of the image upon which you are focused. If, on the other hand, you find that the mind starts becoming more chaotic with an abundance of thoughts, then you should lower the gaze to the Buddha's navel center or seat or to the lower part of the object, trying to relax. If the mind becomes chaotic, too much effort is being applied. If there seems to be no extreme reaction and things are progressing fairly well, then you can maintain your view at the heart center of the image.

This stage of the practice may be maintained for however long is necessary, until you are able to maintain your concentration for an extended period of time without the distraction of disturbing thoughts.

When you are tired of using objects or images, then do not think of anything; simply remain in the nature of the mind, without any focus or thought of the past, hope for the future, or contrivance in the present. Just remain in the natural state of the mind as it is. If you are able to maintain quiescence when there is no elaboration or focus, then that is good. The method that is taught according to the root text is to use a seed syllable. Here, the syllable HUM is visualized in the center of the heart and is about the size of one's thumbnail, red in color. When you become aware of the HUM, you should not try to grab hold of it with your mind, especially to the point where you are holding onto its size, color and other details of its characteristics. Instead, you should just simply acknowledge the presence of HUM, allowing it to be there.

After that, if you find that you are a bit distracted and you need another technique, again you may try to focus upon an object in the space in front. Allow your gaze and mind to mingle with the object, whether it's a stone, a stick, or a flower. Your eyes should not be shifting from side to side – in fact, your eyebrows shouldn't even be moving. Your gaze should be motionless.

Whatever you are focusing upon, your mind must be upon that, not just your visual perception. If you are using an object in the space in front of you, visually you are perceiving it. With your mind, you must cognize it, and there must be no other distractions. After practicing this way for even a short period of time in the beginning, you *will* become distracted; you *will* become tired. You will start to become mentally agitated, or you will become dull and sleepy. These are both distractions. What do you do? You may shout, "Phat!" in order to cut through the distractions and put your mind and vision back on the right track. You may straighten up your body again and turn your gaze upward. If you are having a lot of distracted thoughts, you may take that distracted thought and just apply it to your meditative object. At this point in the practice, you may actually take the thought that you have been chasing and force it into the object that you are focusing upon in the space in front of you, in order to bring your attention back to the object.

Just as you may be distracted by different thoughts, you may also be distracted by other sensual experiences, such as sound. As you hear a sound, if it's pleasing to you, rather than pursuing the sound because of your attraction, recognize that its nature is empty and allow it to dissolve into the empty nature, and maintain your meditation. If it is an unpleasant sound that you dislike, it's no different from the pleasant one. Your mind may also be distracted by a smell, a feeling, or a sensation. As soon as you can, become aware that you've become distracted by that sensual experience. Realize that that experience is of the nature of emptiness. Let it dissolve into its empty origin and return to your meditation.

When you are able to work through some of these coarse distractions, slowly, slowly through your practice, you will begin to become aware of discursive thoughts that you have never been aware of before. The obvious distractions would have already surfaced, right from the very beginning; but then those thoughts that you have never been aware of, that you cannot remember ever even having, new memories, and previously unrecalled events will emerge. In fact, you may feel as though you are losing your mind.

The important thing to remember is that these discursive thoughts are not new. They are very old. The mind is like dirty water that's been stirred up so that all the mud and silt that would otherwise settle to the bottom remains at the surface. When the mind begins to settle down, like the mud naturally settling to the bottom, you are able to observe characteristics that you were not aware of before. In fact, those characteristics of your delusion have always been there and must be dealt with as well.

When these thoughts arise, it doesn't matter whether they seem to be good or bad. On this level of practice, there is no difference between good thoughts and bad thoughts. Thoughts are thoughts. What you must do is recognize them as thought formations that are arising, and as soon as you identify them with indifference, they will dissolve. After you practice this way for some time, you will certainly begin to experience physical and mental bliss to the point where you will not want to get up from the meditation cushion. The meditation will be far more comfortable to you than what you do the rest of the time. You will want to remain practicing indefinitely.

At this point, there are two experiences that arise during quiescence. The first is the experience of physical and mental bliss and a feeling that you never want to stop meditating. This experience is still impure. Here in your meditation experience you may no longer experience the sense fields of form, sound, sight, taste, and touch. It is somewhat like entering into a deep sleep. You do not really know what's going on around you; you cannot hear things; you cannot see things; you cannot feel things, smell, taste, etc. When you arise from meditation, it is similar to awakening from a very deep sleep. You do not know what happened or where the time went. This is the experience of impure quiescence, because you are unable to recall what happens during the experience. It is almost as though the mind goes into a blank state. This is not liberation, nor is it the ultimate result. This is, however, a stage in the experience. Why? Because it is a sign that you are beginning to accomplish quiescence and that the mind is able to remain still for a duration of time without the disturbance of mental afflictions. If you become attached to this as the ultimate experience, you will take rebirth again in cyclic existence. Without attachment you must move on in your practice, knowing that there is much more to come.

Pure quiescence is the next step in the experience of remaining in a state of single-pointed concentration for an indefinite period of time. Here there is tremendous clarity. Although the mind is still, it is lucid and clear. There is total recollection of the experience throughout the meditation and in the post-meditative experience.

During the initial stage of impure quiescence, the eight cognitive states[1] are obstructed while in meditation. As one proceeds to the experience of pure quiescence, clarity is unobstructed since the sensory experiences function normally yet the mind never wavers from single-pointed absorption.

While meditating there is the freedom to be in the experience of single-pointed concentration at any given time and in any way. The conclusion of formal meditation would not constitute the termination of quiescence because the power of the state of awareness would permeate the post-meditative experience of daily life activities.

How long does it take to achieve pure quiescence? This kind of experience comes as the result of tremendous effort in practice. This is not a result that comes easily or quickly.

Other benefits of this accomplishment include physical and mental exhilaration; and since there is no distraction, the practice can then be carried out indefinitely. Right now when you practice, both mind and body tire easily; and, as you become uncomfortable, you switch to something else in order to change the experience of discomfort. Upon arriving at the level of pure quiescence, the body and mind are always in a state of comfort. However, if the mind attaches to the experience of feeling mental and physical bliss, then that mind of attachment will begin to produce the causes for rebirth in the desire realm, bringing you right back into cyclic existence again. There must never be attachment to any experience.

Generally you should keep in mind that, when your meditation practice begins to deepen, there are three experiences that will occur. The first is bliss, the second is clarity, and the third is the experience of having no thoughts. When you have these experiences, if you allow yourself to attach to the experience thinking that somehow you've achieved the ultimate result, then you will be producing causes for rebirth in samsara once again. Do not mistake these experiences for the ultimate result of enlightenment. If you attach to bliss, you will be establishing the causes for rebirth in the desire realm. If you become attached to luminosity or clarity, this establishes causes for rebirth in the form realm. Attachment to no thoughts establishes causes for rebirth in the formless god realm. These are the three realms (desire, form, and formless) of cyclic existence within which the six classes of beings revolve. Through meditation, you can actually produce causes for rebirth in those three realms of existence if you are not careful.

This is a concise explanation of how to practice to accomplish quiescence which includes advice on what to be aware of while practicing. If you are able to practice successfully, you will achieve quiescence for extended periods of time and meditate with clarity, thus preparing you for the second phase, the main practice of cultivating the primordial wisdom of insight.

The teachings and practice of developing the primordial wisdom of insight have two approaches. The first is the approach of scholastic training in order to ascertain the empty nature of the mind. Here, emptiness is ascertained through analytical investigation, eventually proving it to be void of true inherent existence. This view of emptiness is based on intellectual understanding. The second approach is to ascertain the nature of emptiness through the depth of one's practice. This view of emptiness is based on internal realization. If one is able to realize emptiness according to the second approach, then the first is unnecessary.

If you wish to pursue the first approach through scholastic training and then apply that to the practical application of meditation, this is most excellent and is the way that many great practitioners have approached the path. However, at this time in your lives, you should also consider that you might not have many years to practice, since the time of death is uncertain. Furthermore, with such busy lifestyles, the opportunities for practicing meditation are few. It might be better to directly engage in practice in order to get results more quickly.

These days it seems almost everyone is more interested in push-button techniques that work quickly, bringing instant results. Naturally everyone wants the swiftest results. If you think that you can find a push-button experience on the spiritual path, then it means that you have got to practice and meditate, not just listen to the teaching, not just think about it later on, but sit down and really practice. Oftentimes people just listen to dharma, think about it occasionally, and don't practice. How can there be results if there is no practice?

It is through the experience of insight that the primordial wisdom nature of mind is actualized. There are four stages to this development. The first is achieving confidence in the view; the second, experiencing the meditation. The meditation *must* be experienced; it cannot be just an intellectual pursuit. Otherwise it's like a patch that is placed over a hole to cover it. At some time or another, the patch will fall off. Intellectual understanding is impermanent and subject to change. Realization achieved through meditation is permanent. The third stage is sustaining continuity with behavior in daily life activities, and the fourth is actualizing the ultimate result.

First, to achieve confidence in the view, there are three parts. The first is to establish the nature of objects which are apprehended as external. The second is to establish awareness of the nature of the mind which is the internal apprehender. The third is to ascertain the view of the nature of reality.

The first stage of establishing the nature of objects which are apprehended as external involves awareness of how the mind grasps onto external objects as truly existing. This refers to all objective appearances that are perceived outside of the self. All such appearances are grasped onto by the subjective mind as truly existing. Due to this, many scholars will dissect objective appearances into atomic particles and then into nothingness, thus coming to understand that their nature is void of true existence. According to this system, objective phenomena arise from the mind and exist in the mind of the apprehender. Although you think that objective appearances truly exist, the inanimate and animate world would not exist if it were not for the mind. Failing to recognize the mind's nature and allowing the mind to remain in the experience of confused perception, you actually believe that objective appearances are true just as they are perceived. It then becomes very difficult to accept that objective appearances do not have true, inherent existence and are created by the mind.

The first problem is that your mind is in the experience of confused perception. The second is the truth of impermanence, in that there is nothing that the mind perceives, including itself, that is permanent and that can be held onto as true or real. Since everything is subject to change, this implies that there is no true inherent existence, because the nature of phenomena is impermanent. The dream you had last night is no longer true today. At the time you were dreaming, it seemed to be very true, very real. Where is it now? What happened?

To give another analogy, a magician who is skilled in the manipulation of appearances is able to create a magical illusion through the use of substances and mantras, all the while knowing that the appearance he creates is not real. Those who view the magic display think it is real. Perhaps an elephant, tiger or bird came out of the hat and, as it is perceived, it is believed to true; however, the magician knows it is merely an illusion.

Similarly, all objective appearances are nothing more than mental labels. You can say, "This is a table. This is a house." Each one of these objects has its name because it appears to you to be that object. Therefore, you have a label for it. In truth, its nature is illusory and it doesn't really exist any more than the illusory appearance that a magician creates. Therefore, you must have confidence in the primordial wisdom awareness of the illusory nature of all appearances. Through this you are able to establish the nature of objects which are apprehended as external.

This leads you to the second step in the practice of developing insight, which is establishing the nature of the mind as the internal apprehender. The creator of objective appearances is the subject, the mind itself. If you try to locate the mind, can you find its location? Can you determine its characteristics? Can it be found to be substantial or tangible? According to the many systems of Buddhist thought, there are countless techniques that may be employed to discover the origin of the mind to determine if it truly exists or not.

In order to engage in the formal practice, first of all you should sit in the correct meditation posture. Allow the speech to remain silent and breathe naturally. Do not force the mind to be too tense or too slack; just remain relaxed in your own pure awareness nature.

Sometimes as you sit, it may occur to you that there are two processes occurring: that of apprehending the mind and that of apprehending the apprehender. If you notice this, then allow the apprehender to look at the apprehending mind, which is like observing one's own face directly without anything else in between. When you become aware in this way, you will begin to realize that the apprehender and apprehending mind are non-dual. Then you will realize that the object being apprehended by the apprehender and the mind apprehending it are all indivisible, the same experience. Thereby, you can come to see that the object and the subject, the grasping and clinging, are no longer dual. It is one experience, which is the nature of the mind, free from any limitations of contrived mental activity. What happens then if there is no subject and no object? Then what do you have? All you have is the experience of your own innate buddha nature. In the initial stages of the practice, you will experience this state free from duality for a fleeting instant. In the second moment, dualistic grasping and clinging will resume. These days there are many who spend a considerable amount of time sitting in silent meditation. If you know how to practice the generation or completion stage and have actually established the view with confidence so as to be able to ascertain the nature of emptiness, then extended periods of silent meditation can be extremely illuminating. However, if you have no training or experience and just sit there silently with surges of turbulent concepts and mental distractions, it is just a waste of time.

During the experience of non-duality, allow yourself to remain in the freshness of the experience, without any contrived alterations. A practitioner with superior intelligence will be able to remain in this experience of intrinsic awareness indefinitely. In the beginning, it is difficult to remain for very long. This experience is, however, identical to the experience you have in between thoughts. When the first thought ends and before the second thought begins, the fresh moment in between is identical to the experience of intrinsic awareness. The reason you are not aware of that now is because you have so many thoughts arising so quickly that the moment in between them remains unnoticed.

Maybe you will think the moment in between thoughts is a dull state similar to the experience of impure quiescence. In the experience of the moment between thoughts, all eight cognitive states are functioning normally. The mind is luminously clear and able to cognize anything, yet totally void of duality because there is no presence of thought formations or deluded mental activity. If you have understood this, it means you have had a glimpse of the general experience of intrinsic awareness.

Why, then, do you as ordinary individuals have such a difficult time recognizing this general experience of your own primordial wisdom nature? This is primarily due to the intensity of habituation to duality and discursive thoughts. Due to that you are defeated time and time again by your own conceptualizations. In addition, in the past you have heard instructions about the nature of the mind but have failed to practice. Then, what method can you employ since you are so distracted by your own mind? The method is to try to search for the source of the mind, the creator of discursive thoughts, the root cause of all of your problems.

You've already been able to come to terms with the fact that concepts arise from the mind. Now you must find where the mind originates, where it exists, and where it finally ceases. Similarly, try to understand where discursive thoughts originate, where they exist, and where they cease.

Where does the experience of enlightenment originate, exist, and cease? Where does the experience of samsara originate, exist, and cease? Who experiences bliss and suffering? If you come to the conclusion that it is the mind that experiences enlightenment and samsara, then from where does the mind originate, exist, and cease? Is it tangible or not? Is it formless?

If you determine that the mind has a form, then you should try to determine what shape and color it is. If it is tangible, it must possess some characteristics. If you think that it is void of any substantial existence, then you should try to examine what that experience is. It is essential to have a spiritual teacher who has already realized the nature of the mind who can help to accurately guide you through this experience. A qualified spiritual teacher on this level of practice is one who has ascertained the nature of the mind. In Tibet there are many instances where disciples were led astray by teachers with no realization. On this level of practice, there are many dangers and pitfalls.

If, through the process of examination, you are totally unable to find the mind and what you have found instead is just like the sphere of space itself – open, like looking into a vast, empty space – yet you are unable to express it, then you are on the right track. However, this experience of voidness is not the negation of everything, falling to the extreme of nihilism, believing there is nothing. It is an experience that is very open; and, within that openness, there are many, many possibilities. It is also important to be very careful about the depth of these teachings. If you take them literally, without any meditative experience, there is the danger of becoming confused about reality and losing your sanity. This is why it's important to receive teachings under the guidance of a qualified teacher according to the tradition. Through this tradition, enlightenment can be realized in one body and in one lifetime, because these teachings have the power to establish practitioners in the state of liberation where there is permanent freedom from all traces of confused perception. Knowing the nature of the mind is really the pith point of the entire path; however, it can also be very dangerous if you do not approach it carefully and correctly.

The third step is ascertaining the view of the nature of reality. According to this rediscovered treasure from the wrathful emanation of Guru Rinpoche, Dorje Drolö, open luminosity is the nature of Dorje Drolö. This refers to the nature of the mind of all buddhas, which is the nature of all meditative deities, of all lamas, dakinis, and true objects of refuge. In order to realize that nature, you do not need to search any place other than within yourselves. That nature is the essence of your mind and is a self-originating experience. Realize that it pervasively encompasses all that constitutes samsara and nirvana. The mind of all the buddhas, your own innate nature, is the experience of primordial wisdom, free from duality, luminously clear, unobstructedly compassionate.

After you have achieved confidence in the view, you can then gain the experience of meditation as the deepening of the view. Remaining free from the thoughts of the past, present, or future, poised in unmediated, fresh awareness is also referred to as the meditation. This luminous, open experience, which is the self-originating nature of one's mind, does not need to be searched for as a separate meditation experience. You should not consider that you're trying to create an artificial experience. It is simply recognizing and remaining directly introduced to your own nature.

This is the meaning of the dharmakaya (embodiment of ultimate reality). Furthermore, in this dharmakaya experience, sensual perceptions are present and are simply observed impartially, without any dualistic grasping or clinging. This openness is luminously clear and encompasses everything, without suffering, because there is no duality. It cannot benefit, and it cannot harm. It goes beyond the realm of benefit and harm, acceptance or rejection. You no longer need to think, "Oh, I can't do that; I must not do that."

The third step is to sustain continuity with one's behavior. Conduct must be like the meditation, and

the meditation must be like the view. Each one sub-
sumes the other. Usually you consider that conduct is
a post-meditative experience that occurs after your
formal session. To sustain continuity with conduct is
to integrate the view, meditation, and conduct indivisibly.

Since the meditative equipoise is simply remaining
in open, unmediated intrinsic awareness, unspoiled
by grasping and clinging, totally luminous and relaxed, when you arise from that experience, you
should perceive all appearances and experiences to
be like an illusory display of the intrinsic awareness
nature. All form is seen as the meditational deity,
divine form. You may hear the essence of all sound to
be that of mantra. All thoughts are understood as the
play of pure awareness. You may also consider that
appearances in daily life are like a dream, an illusion,
with no true inherent existence.

On this level of practice, there is no distinction
between the meditation and conduct. The meditative
experience is to be carried into the way one perceives
daily life appearances and conducts oneself. This
means that discursive thoughts would be utilized as
the appearance of the path, rather than a hindrance.
When grasping and clinging ceases, thoughts arise as
an illusion to adorn the path.

If, perhaps, you still think that a discursive thought
is harming you, bringing some pain or problem, just
enter into it and see that it is empty in nature and it will
dissolve. If you pursue the thought and thereby allow
it to control the mind, then you have lost the view.
Otherwise, if you absorb into the thought, you will see
that the nature is empty and it will dissolve, like the

waves that well up in the ocean and disappear back into the ocean. There's nothing wrong with a discursive thought arising, when you realize that it arises from pure awareness and dissolves back into pure awareness.

When you are able to recognize that discursive thoughts are none other than the display of intrinsic awareness itself, empty and void of true inherent existence, you will let go of them and watch them dissolve back into their empty source. In brief, you must be careful, in this practice of conduct as the path, not to become disturbed by distractions and overpowered by your habituation to grasping and clinging. As a practitioner, your practice should be like a flowing river – unceasing and steady.

The fourth and final step is the manner in which fruition is achieved. Fruition is the recognition of one's own originally pure, intrinsic awareness nature, free from confusion. This experience, which is the result of the view, meditation, and conduct, is the experience of enlightenment or ultimate freedom from the confusion of cyclic existence. If your practice is strong, then even before your death, by realizing this nature and actualizing it according to these four steps, you will be liberated. Otherwise, liberation will occur at the moment of your death or in the bardo state. Through the blessings of accomplishing this practice, it is certain that liberation will occur during one of these times.

It is imperative to have strong faith in your primary teacher, the teacher who introduces you to the nature of the mind, so that you can recognize your own nature. These are the pith instructions for success in this practice. The ultimate result of quiescence, primordial wisdom insight, mahamudra and mahasandhi, is nothing other than this.

Notes

PART I   TRANSFORMATION

Part 2: Commentary

(1) The five mental afflictions are impure awareness, aggression-hatred, pride, desire-attachment, and jealousy.

(2) The eight worldly concerns are to practice dharma for gain, loss, pleasure, misery, praise, degradation, fame, or fear of blame.

(3) The preliminary practices include six common contemplations and six uncommon practices. The six common contemplations are the precious human rebirth and how difficult it is to obtain, the impermanence of life and existence, the truth of the law of cause and result, the suffering of cyclic existence, how to rely upon a qualified spiritual teacher, and the benefits of liberation. The six uncommon practices are refuge-bodhicitta, mandala, Vajrasattva, guru yoga, chöd (exorcism of self-grasping), and phowa (transference of consciousness).

PART III   MEDITATION

Part 1: Root Text

(1) Pronounced "hoong."

(2) Dorje Drolö.

Part 2: Commentary

(1) The eight cognitive states are eye consciousness, ear consciousness, nose consciousness, tongue consciousness, body consciousness, mental consciousness, afflicted consciousness and foundation consciousness or mind basis of all.